MOSCOW
architecture & design

Edited by Katharina Feuer
Written by Irina Chipova, Katharina Feuer
Concept by Martin Nicholas Kunz

teNeues

content

introduction 6

to see . living

to see . office

to see . culture & education

to see . public

content

to stay . hotels

to go . eating, drinking, clubbing

to go . wellness, beauty & sport

to shop . mall, retail, showrooms

introduction

Yakut Gallery at Gasholder

Villa Ostozhenka

The vibrantly colored mixture of different periods and styles, national traditions and global culture, of provinciality and the chic of a sophisticated metropolis influences the Russian capital's image. Its contemporary architecture is just as bright and diverse as Moscow itself—from refined minimalism to color-happy post-modernism, from deconstructivism to neo-classicism. Discover the same variety in the design of numerous boutiques, cafés, and restaurants und hotels.

Nowadays, you can realize the most ambitious projects in Moscow, for example Federation Tower or Russia Tower, and that is precisely why this city is a magnet for international architects and designers.

Die bunte Mischung aus verschiedenen Epochen und Stilen, aus nationalen Traditionen und globaler Kultur, aus Provinzialität und dem Chic einer mondänen Metropole prägt das Bild der russischen Hauptstadt. Genau wie Moskau selbst, so bunt und vielfältig ist seine heutige Architektur – von raffiniertem Minimalismus bis farbenfroher Postmoderne, vom Dekonstruktivismus bis zur Neoklassik. Die gleiche Vielfalt entdeckt man im Design der zahlreichen Boutiquen, Cafés, Restaurants und Hotels.

In Moskau kann man heutzutage die ambitioniertesten Projekte verwirklichen, wie beispielsweise den Federation Tower oder den Russia Tower, und gerade deswegen ist diese Stadt ein Magnet für Architekten und Designer aus aller Welt.

Panorama

Le mélange bigarré d'époques et de styles différents, de traditions nationales et de culture mondiale, de régionalisme et d'originalité propre à une métropole mondaine, caractérise l'aspect de la capitale russe. Son architecture actuelle est aussi multicolore et variée que la ville même – allant du minimalisme raffiné au postmodernisme chamarré, du déconstructivisme au néoclassicisme. La même diversité se retrouve dans le design de ses nombreux magasins, cafés, restaurants et hôtels.

A Moscou, il est possible aujourd'hui de réaliser les projets les plus ambitieux, tels que la Federation Tower ou la Russia Tower ; c'est bien pourquoi cette ville magnétise les architectes et les designers du monde entier.

Swissôtel Krasnye Holrny

La capital rusa está envuelta de una multicolor mezcla de diversas épocas y estilos, tradiciones nacionales y cultura global, un carácter provincial y el aire chic típico de una metrópoli mundana. Y tan diversa y colorida como la ciudad misma es su arquitectura actual: desde el minimalismo refinado hasta un postmodernismo rico en colores, desde el desconstructivismo hasta el neoclasicismo. Una amplia paleta que se hace igualmente patente en el diseño de las numerosas boutiques, cafés, restaurantes y hoteles.

Hoy en Moscú es posible hacer realidad los proyectos más ambiciosos, como acreditan la Federation Tower y la Russia Tower, de ahí que la ciudad se haya convertido en un verdadero imán que atrae a arquitectos y diseñadores de todo el mundo.

Living Complex Molochniy Lane

to see . living
office
culture & education
public

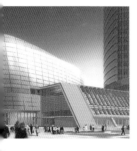

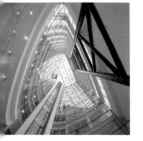

Pompeii House

M. Belov

2005
Filippovsky Lane 13
Arbat

The cheerful colors, fabulous décor, multi-colored ledges, and columns growing out of flowers are inspired by Pompeian frescos, but their location next to a Moscow church from the 17th century makes them seem organic; it's as if they originate from the same time and are part of the same style.

Die fröhlichen Farben und das märchenhafte Dekor, die bunten Gesimse und die aus Blumen wachsenden Säulen sind von pompejischen Fresken inspiriert, wirken aber neben der Moskauer Kirche des 17. Jahrhunderts so organisch, als stammen sie aus der selben Zeit und gehören zum gleichen Stil.

Les couleurs gaies d'un décor de conte de fées, les corniches colorées et les colonnes jaillissant de corolles de fleurs sont inspirées des fresques de Pompeï ; pourtant, à côté de l'église moscovite du 17ème siècle, elles ont l'air tellement organiques qu'on les croirait issues de la même époque et du même style.

Los alegres colores, decoración de fábula, molduras multicolores y flores abriéndose en columnas, se inspiran en los frescos de Pompeya, si bien, al lado de la iglesia del siglo XVII crean un efecto tan orgánico que parecen provenir de la misma época y estilo.

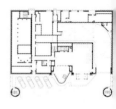

Stolnik

Architectural Bureau A-B, A. Savin, M. Labazov, A. Tscheltsov
Alexander Botschkov (SE)

2002
Maly Lewschinsky Lane 2
Arbat

This extravagant townhouse breaks with all the conventions of its location and provides a stunning visual centerpiece for the street. Its pointedly modern high-tech façades, however, hide bourgeois premises with fine wood and stone cladding reminiscent of art deco.

Dieses extravagante Wohnhaus bricht mit allen Konventionen des Ortes und zieht alle Blicke auf sich. Doch hinter den betont modernen Hightech-Fassaden verbergen sich bourgeoise Räumlichkeiten mit edlen Holz- und Steinverkleidungen, die an das Art déco erinnern.

Cet immeuble résidentiel extravagant rompt avec toutes les conventions du lieu et attire sur lui tous les regards. Pourtant, derrière les façades haute technologie résolument modernes se cachent des demeures bourgeoises avec des revêtements de pierre et de bois précieux qui rappellent le style Art Déco.

Este extravagante edificio de viviendas rompe con todas las convenciones del lugar y atrae a todas las miradas. Pero tras la marcada fachada de línea alta tecnología se esconden estancias burguesas con revestimientos de piedra y maderas nobles que evocan el estilo Art Déco.

Townhouses Zachatyevskiy Lane

Ostozhenka Architects, A. Skokan, R. Baishev, O. Fridland, I. Voronezhskiy, K. Gladkiy, M. Elizarova

2002
Zachatyevskiy Lane 1
Ostozhenka

www.ostarch.ru

The façades of 17 modern townhouses situated on a joint platform flank an alleyway inside the block. Despite the creative complexity of the structure, it appears outwardly consistent owing to its winter gardens, which are similar among all house types.

Die Fassaden von 17 modernen Stadthäusern, die auf eine gemeinsame Plattform gestellt sind, flankieren eine Gasse im Blockinneren. Trotz der gestalterischen Vielfalt des Komplexes, wirkt er dank der bei allen Haustypen ähnlichen Wintergärten einheitlich.

Les façades de ces 17 maisons d'habitation modernes, édifiées sur une plate-forme commune, longent une ruelle au sein du pâté de maisons. Malgré la diversité dans la conception du complexe, celui-ci paraît homogène grâce aux jardins d'hiver identiques pour tous les types de maison.

Las fachadas de 17 casas urbanas, levantadas sobre una plataforma común flanquean una callejuela del interior del bloque. A pesar de la diversidad con la que está concebido el complejo, los jardines de invierno que contienen cada uno de los tipos de casa hacen que se mantenga el estilo unitario.

Villa Ostozhenka

Meganom, Yurj Grigoryan, Alexandra Pavlova, Pavel Ivantchikov, Ilja Kuleshov
M. Kelman (SE)

2004
Molochniy Lane 1
Ostozhenka

This unique residence made of concrete and glass has an underground winter garden and a "swimming aquarium" made of glass. It is a social as well as an architectural experiment as the first family residence built in the middle of the city since the 1917 revolution.

Die einzigartige Villa aus Beton und Glas mit einem unterirdischen Wintergarten und einem gläsernen „Schwimm-Aquarium" ist nicht nur ein architektonisches, sondern auch ein soziales Experiment, als das erste, seit der Revolution von 1917 mitten in der Stadt erbaute Einfamilienhaus.

Cette villa unique, de béton et de verre, avec un jardin d'hiver souterrain et un « aquarium flottant » en verre, ne constitue pas seulement une expérience architecturale mais aussi sociale, dans la mesure où il s'agit de la première habitation individuelle construite en pleine ville depuis la révolution de 1917.

La exclusiva villa de hormigón y vidrio, con un jardín de invierno subterráneo y un "acuario-piscina" acristalado, es no sólo un experimento arquitectónico sino a la vez social, puesto que se trata de la primera vivienda familiar construida en el centro de la ciudad, desde la revolución de 1917.

Living Complex
Molochniy Lane

Meganom, Yurj Grigoryan, Alexandra Pavlova, Pavel Ivantchikov, Ilja Kuleshov
M. Kelman (SE)

2003
Molochniy Lane 3
Ostozhenka

The elegantly rounded façade with its bright limestone and glass gallery surrounds a small park, making it a place where the line between private and public space blurs. The house appears solemn, yet open and clear.

Die elegant gerundete Fassade mit hellem Kalkstein und der gläsernen Galerie umrahmt einen kleinen Park. Hier verschwimmt die Grenze zwischen privatem und öffentlichem Raum. Das Haus wirkt repräsentativ, gleichzeitig aber offen und klar.

L'élégante façade en courbe avec de la pierre à chaux claire et une galerie vitrée encadre un petit parc. Ici, la frontière entre espace privé et public s'estompe. La maison est représentative, conservant simultanément un aspect ouvert et clair.

Esta elegante fachada ondulada de caliza clara y una galería acristalada rodea un pequeño parque. Aquí se difuminan los límites entre el espacio privado y el público. El edificio tiene un aspecto representativo, pero al mismo tiempo claro y abierto.

Crystal House

Meganom, Yurj Grigoryan, Alexandra Pavlova, Pavel Ivanschikov, Ilja Kuleshov

2005
Korobeynikov Lane 6, 15, 17
Ostozhenka

The long, natural-stone street façade is contrasted by the three glass cubes placed on a common foundation inside the block. Their curtain wall is made of tinted glass and makes them glisten like crystals, allowing one to see them from as far as the other bank of the Moskva.

Den Kontrast zur langen, natursteinverkleideten Straßenfassade bilden die drei auf einen gemeinsamen Sockel gesetzten gläsernen Kuben im Blockinneren. Dank der Vorhangfassade aus getöntem Glas glitzern sie wie Kristalle, die man bereits vom anderen Ufer der Moskwa aus sehen kann.

Les trois cubes de verre placés sur un socle commun, dans le pâté de maison, créent le contraste avec la longue façade revêtue de pierre naturelle, donnant sur la rue. Grâce à leur façade-rideau de verre teinté, ils scintillent comme des cristaux que l'on aperçoit de loin, de l'autre rive de la Moskova.

La extensa fachada de la calle revestida de piedra natural crea contraste con los tres cubos de vidrio que se levantan sobre una base común en el interior del bloque. La fachada de cortina de vidrio tintado resplandece como un cristal de cuarzo visible desde la otra orilla del Moskwa.

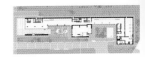

Copper House

Sergej Skuratov Architects, Sergej Skuratov
M. Kelman (SE)

2003
Butikovsky Lane 3
Ostozhenka

www.skuratov-arch.ru

The three volumes of the complex are linked by a narrow glass gallery, which appears as a backdrop for the small inner courtyards. With its façade of tinted glass and patinated copper, the house blends into the landscape of the riverbank while still retaining its modern, urban appearance.

Die drei Baukörper des Komplexes verbindet eine schmale gläserne Galerie, die wie eine Kulisse für die kleinen Innenhöfe wirkt. Dank der Fassadenverkleidung aus getöntem Glas und patiniertem Kupfer fügt sich das Haus organisch in die Uferlandschaft ein, wirkt dabei aber trotzdem städtisch und modern.

Les trois volumes du complexe sont reliés par une étroite galerie de verre qui constitue une coulisse pour les petites cours intérieures. Grâce au revêtement de façade en verre teinté et au cuivre patiné, la maison s'intègre de façon organique dans le paysage des bords de la rivière, tout en restant urbaine et moderne.

Los tres volumenes del complejo enlazan una estrecha galería de vidrio, que parece el decorado de los patios interiores. Gracias al revestimiento de la fachada en vidrio tintado y cobre patinado, el edificio se funde de forma orgánica en el paisaje que envuelve a las orillas del río, sin dejar por ello de desprender un carácter moderno y urbano.

House at Butikovsky Lane

Sergej Skuratov Architects, Sergej Skuratov
M. Kelman (SE)

2003
Butikovsky Lane 5
Ostozhenka

www.skuratov-arch.ru

This home's great façade structure—with its contrast between bright Jurassic limestone and dark clinkers as well as its asymmetrical composition—make the residence seem like an ensemble of various volumes. Here, the tradition of the Ostozhenka quarter is translated into modern forms.

Dank der plastischen Fassadengliederung, dem Kontrast zwischen hellem Jurakalkstein und dunklen Klinkern und der Asymmetrie der Komposition wirkt das Haus als ein Ensemble unterschiedlicher Volumina. Damit wird die Tradition des Viertels Ostozhenka in moderne Formen übersetzt.

Grâce à l'articulation plastique de la façade, au contraste entre la pierre à chaux jurassique et les briques sombres et à l'asymétrie de la composition, la maison semble constituer un ensemble aux volumes différents. Ceci permet de traduire en formes modernes la tradition du quartier d'Ostozhenka.

La estructuración plástica, el contraste entre la piedra caliza blanca, los clincker oscuros y la composición asimétrica dan a la casa un efecto de conjunto de volúmenes diversos. Con ello, la tradición del barrio Ostozhenka se traduce ahora en formas modernas.

Patriarch

Sergej Tkatschenko, V. Belskiy, I. Voznesenskiy, A. Kononenko, M. Liykin
E.Spivak, V. Gnedin, E. Skatchkova (SE)

2003
Ermolaevskiy Lane 15/44
Patriarch's Pond

www.sbtkachenko.ru

A capriccio of all forms of architecture that do justice to the idea of a "Moscow Style" is crowned by a paraphrase on Vladimir Tatlin's Monument to the Third International. The residence owes its name to the Patriarch Pond, located nearby.

Ein Capriccio aus allen Architekturformen, die der Vorstellung eines „Moskauer Stils" entsprechen, wird von einer Paraphrase auf Wladimir Tatlins „Monument der III. Internationale" gekrönt. Seinen Namen hat das Gebäude von dem nahe gelegenen Patriarchen-Teich.

Un capriccio de toutes les formes architecturales qui répondent à l'idée que l'on se fait d'un « style moscovite » est couronné ici par une paraphrase sur la « Tour de la 3ème Internationale » de Vladimir Tatlin. Le bâtiment doit son nom à l'étang du Patriarche situé à proximité.

Un capricho que envuelve todas las formas arquitectónicas integrantes de la imagen del "estilo Moscovita", como una paráfrasis que evoca el "Monumento a la Tercera Internacional" de Vladimir Tatlin. El edificio debe su nombre al vecino estanque de los patriarcas.

Fabergé-Egg House

S. Tkachenko, O. Dubrovskiy, I. Voznesenskiy, A. Kononenko
E. Skatchkova, A. Litvinova, N. Kosjmina (SE)

2002
Maschkova Street 1/11
Pokrovka

www.sbtkachenko.ru

This distinctive four-story house, designed to resemble a multi-colored Fabergé Egg, humorously explores architectural allusions ranging from baroque to art nouveau. It was designed as an eye-catcher for a conventional housing estate.

Das auffällige vierstöckige Haus, das an ein farbenfrohes Fabergé-Ei erinnern soll, spielt humorvoll mit Architekturzitaten von Barock bis Jugendstil. Es wurde als Blickfang für einen konventionellen Wohnkomplex konzipiert.

Cette maison frappante de quatre étages, censée rappeler un œuf de Fabergé aux couleurs vives, met en œuvre avec humour des citations architecturales allant du baroque à l'Art nouveau. Elle a pour but d'attirer le regard sur un complexe résidentiel conventionnel.

El llamativo edificio de cuatro plantas, que pretende recordar a un huevo Fabergé de colores alegres, juega con humor con elementos arquitectónicos que abarcan desde el barroco hasta el modernismo. Fue concebido como punto de atención en un complejo de viviendas convencional.

Panorama

Ostozhenka Architects, A. Skokan, V. Kanyshin, M. Dekhtyar, M.Kudrjashov
S. Schatz (SE)

2004
Presnensky Val 14
Presnya

www.ostarh.ru

A façade mosaic made of glass gives this housing complex a graceful appearance and creates a multitude of optical effects. The building was divided into two asymmetrical parts with a narrow, curvilinear cut that allows for a view of the church in the background from the street.

Ein gläsernes Fassadenmosaik vermittelt diesem Komplex Leichtigkeit und schafft vielfältige optische Effekte. Das Haus wurde durch einen schmalen, gekrümmten Schnitt in zwei asymmetrische Teile gespalten, um von der Straße aus einen Blick auf die Kirche im Hintergrund zu ermöglichen.

Une mosaïque de façades de verre confère à ce complexe une grande légèreté et crée une multitude d'effets d'optique. Une étroite coupe incurvée divise l'immeuble en deux parties asymétriques, ce qui ouvre la vue, de la rue, sur l'église à l'arrière-plan.

El mosaico acristalado que forma la fachada transmite al complejo un aire de ligereza y crea numerosos efectos ópticos. La casa fue dividida en dos bloques asimétricos a través de un fino corte curvado, de manera que desde la calle se tuviera una vista de la iglesia de fondo.

House Klimashkina Street

Ostozhenka Architects, A. Skokan, V. Kanyshin, M. Dekhtyar, A. Ass, L. Vintova

2002
Klimashkina Street 13
Presnya

www.ostarh.ru

A small church lies behind this house. To accommodate and frame a view of it, the 15-story residential building was divided in two and its upper stories reconnected with a bridge. This gives the high-rise a new dimension and makes it reminiscent of El Lissitzky's Cloud-Iron.

Hinter dem Haus befindet sich eine kleine Kirche. Um den Blick auf sie zu ermöglichen, wurde das 15-stöckige Wohnhaus zweigeteilt. Die oberen Stockwerke sind dann jedoch wieder durch eine Brücke verbunden. So bekommt das Hochhaus eine neue Dimension und erinnert an El Lissitzkys horizontale Wolkenbügel.

Derrière l'immeuble se trouve une petite église. Pour permettre de la voir, ce bâtiment de 15 étages a été séparé en deux. Les étages supérieurs sont cependant reliés par un pont. L'immeuble revêt ainsi une nouvelle dimension et rappelle l'immeuble horizontal « Wolkenbügel » d'El Lissitzky.

Detrás de la casa se levanta una pequeña iglesia. Con objeto de poder despejar su vista el edificio de 15 plantas fue dividido en dos. Los pisos superiores están a la vez unidos por un puente; de esta manera la estructura adopta una nueva dimensión y asemeja a la nube de hierro horizontal de El Lissitzky.

Catamaran

Reserve, Vladimir Plotkin, Irina Deeva
V. Andreev (SE)

2000
Zagorskogo Passage 11
Kuntsevo

www.reserve.ru

This house consists of two volumes with architectural and color structures that are linked to the tower-like stairwells by small, multi-storied crossings. This complex organization creates a clear composition of four inner courtyards that flow into each other.

Das Haus besteht aus zwei architektonisch und farblich gegliederten Baukörpern, die durch schmale, mehrstöckige Übergänge mit den turmartigen Treppenhäusern verbunden sind. So entsteht eine klare Komposition aus vier ineinander fließenden Innenhöfen.

L'immeuble est constitué de deux corps de bâtiment, distincts par leur architecture et leur couleur, qui sont reliés par d'étroites passerelles sur plusieurs étages avec les cages d'escalier en forme de tours. Il en résulte un assemblage précis de quatre cours intérieures se succédant avec fluidité.

La casa está formada por dos cuerpos de construcción subdivididos en colores que se unen a los edificios en forma de torre a través de pasos estrechos de varios pisos. Con ello se crea una clara composición de cuatro patios interiores que se funden entre sí.

Living Complex
Tatarovskaya Pojma

Reserve, Vladimir Plotkin, Yu. Kuzin
I. Kats, V. Porechny (SE)

2003
Krylatskoe

www.reserve.ru

A state-of-the-art garden city is being created on 63 acres on the banks of the rowing channel. Both its style—combining white cubes or cylinders with ribbon windows, protruding balconies, and roof ledges—and its clearly defined structure are reminiscent of residential estates of the 1920s.

Eine moderne Gartenstadt entsteht auf 25,5 ha an den Ufern des Ruderkanals. Nicht nur die Formsprache von weißen Kuben oder Zylindern mit Fensterbändern, auskragenden Balkonen und Dachbrüstungen, sondern auch die klare Struktur des Komplexes erinnern an Wohnsiedlungen der 20er Jahre.

Une ville jardin moderne est en train de voir le jour sur 25,5 hectares au bord du canal d'aviron. Non seulement le langage des formes, fait de cubes ou de cylindres blancs avec des rangées de fenêtres, des balcons en saillie et des parapets sur les toits, mais aussi la structure précise du complexe rappellent les lotissements d'habitation des années 20.

Una moderna ciudad jardín de 25,5 hectáreas que se abre a orillas del canal de remo. Tanto el lenguaje de formas compuesto de cubos blancos y cilindros con ventanales verticales, balcones de voladizo y armaduras de tejado como la clara estructura del complejo evocan las zonas residenciales de los años 20.

Romanov Dvor 2

Lab for Virtual Architecture, S. Kulish, V. Lipatov, D. Zukov, E. Petrova
(Interior Design), Popov and Architects (Architects)
Yu. Ponamarev (SE)

2004
Romanov Lane 4
Center

www.labva.ru

Transparency, reflectivity, and multiple viewing angles and their interpretations are the prime characteristics of this interior space; these effects are accomplished by means of materials, forms, and a complex display of lights. The impression of numerous perspectives is reinforced by the stairs, which lead in many directions.

Transparenz, Spiegelungen sowie eine Vielfalt der Sichtwinkel und deren Interpretationen sind die wichtigsten Eigenschaften dieses Interieurs, die durch Materialien, Formen und eine komplexe Licht-Regie erreicht werden. Die in verschiedene Richtungen laufenden Treppen verstärken diesen Eindruck.

Transparence, miroitements et diversité des angles de vue avec leurs interprétations sont les caractéristiques principales de cet intérieur, engendrées par les matériaux, les formes et la gestion sophistiquée de la lumière. Les escaliers orientés dans différentes directions renforcent cette impression.

Transparencia, reflejos y multitud de ángulos de visión con diversas interpretaciones son las características principales de este interior, que se define a través de materiales, formas y una intrincada concepción de la luz. La escalera que se abre en varias direcciones acentúa aún más el efecto pretendido.

Penguin

Ostozhenka Architects, A. Skokan, V. Kanyshin, M. Dekhtyar

2005
Brestskaya Street 1
Center

www.ostarch.ru

At first glance, this building looks like a 1960s office high-rise with plain and elegant steel-and-glass façades. Its curvature, however—non-existent in those days—bears the signature of today. The building's name comes from its distinctive silhouette.

Man könnte auf den ersten Blick denken, ein Bürohochhaus der 60er Jahre mit schlichten und eleganten Stahl-Glas-Fassaden vor sich zu sehen. Aber diese Rundung – dergleichen gab es damals noch nicht – das ist eine Geste von heute. Aufgrund seiner markanten Silhouette bekam das Haus den Namen „Pinguin".

A première vue, on pourrait penser qu'on se trouve devant un immeuble de bureaux des années 60 avec ses façades de verre et d'acier, sobres et élégantes. Mais ce galbe – qui n'existait pas comme tel à cette époque – est un geste d'aujourd'hui. Etant donné sa silhouette bien marquée, cet immeuble a été nommé « Le Pingouin ».

A primera vista se podría creer ver un edificio de oficinas de los años 60 con una elegante y sobria fachada de vidrio. Pero esta curvatura no existía entonces; se trata más bien de un motivo actual. El edificio debe su nombre "pingüino" a la marcada silueta.

46

Administrative Building
Kosoy Lane

Ginzburg Architectural Studio, Alexej Ginzburg

2004
Kosoy Lane 23, 3-4
Center

www.ginzburg.ru

This building's clear structure, its combination of vertical and horizontal volumes, and the proportions of ribbon windows that together form an asymmetric composition make visual connections with constructivist architecture of the 1920s inevitable.

Wegen der klaren Struktur, der Kombination von vertikalen und horizontalen Volumina und der Proportionen der Fensterbänder, die eine asymmetrische Komposition bilden, sind die Konnotationen mit der konstruktivistischen Architektur der 20er Jahren bei diesem Gebäude unvermeidbar.

La structure nette, la combinaison de volumes verticaux et horizontaux et les proportions des rangées de fenêtres, créent une composition asymétrique, dont découlent inévitablement, dans le cas de ce bâtiment, des connotations avec l'architecture constructiviste des années 20.

Las estructuras claras, la combinación de volúmenes verticales y horizontales y las proporciones de los ventanales verticales que en su conjunto forman una composición asimétrica, no dejan duda alguna de las connotaciones de la arquitectura constructivista de los años 20 que caracterizan al edificio.

Russian Architectural Union
Reconstruction

A. Asaadov, A. Chernienko, N. Tsymbal, P. Gerasimov
A. Nebytov, G. Vaynshtein, I. Stolyar (SE)

2005
Granatny Lane 22
Center

www.uar.ru
www.asadov.ru

This historic building was razed and reconstructed based on old plans. A green wave of patinated copper has been wrapped around its classic yellow-white façades. These contrasts notwithstanding, it is a place where old and new come together in great harmony.

Das historische Gebäude wurde abgerissen und nach alten Plänen neu gebaut. Seine klassische gelb-weiße Fassade wurde mit einer grünen Welle aus patiniertem Kupfer umhüllt. Trotz aller Kontraste fließen hier Neues und Altes auf sehr harmonische Weise ineinander.

Le bâtiment historique a été démoli et reconstruit suivant les anciens plans. Sa façade classique jaune et blanche a été enveloppée d'une vague verte de cuivre patiné. Malgré tous ces contrastes, l'ancien et le moderne se confondent ici dans une parfaite harmonie.

El edificio histórico fue derrumbado y reconstruido de nuevo según los planos antiguos. Su clásica fachada en tonos amarillos y blancos fue recubierta de una plancha ondulada verde de cobre patinado. A pesar de los contrastes, lo nuevo y lo antiguo se funden de forma armónica.

A-B Architects Office

Architectural Bureau A-B, A. Savin, M. Labazov, A. Tscheltsov

2005
Timura Frunze Street 11/34
Khamovniki

Like its architecture—buoyant, fresh, exciting—so is the office of the architectural group "A-B." The old factory rooms have been painted white from top to bottom. The green plants as well as the room separators and furniture made of transparent, motley glass create a great atmosphere for making designs.

So wie ihre Architektur – jung, frisch, aufregend – ist das Büro der Architektengruppe „A-B". Die alten Fabrikräume wurden von unten bis oben weiß gestrichen, die grünen Pflanzen sowie die Raumteiler und Möbel aus transparentem buntem Glas sorgen für eine gute Atmosphäre beim Entwerfen.

Le bureau du groupe d'architectes « A-B » est à l'image de leur architecture – jeune, rafraîchissante, stimulante. Les locaux d'une ancienne fabrique ont été peints en blanc de haut en bas; les plantes vertes, les cloisons de séparation et les meubles de verre coloré translucide créent une atmosphère de travail agréable pour les architectes.

La oficina del grupo de arquitectos "A–B" es tal y como su arquitectura: joven, fresca y excitante. Las antiguas estancias de una fábrica han sido pintadas en blanco de arriba a abajo. Plantas verdes, espacios de separación y muebles de vidrio transparentes y multicolores se encargan de crear un ambiente agradable que inspira al hacer bosquejos.

Bloomberg News, Moscow

Murray O'Laoire Architects + HLV

2005
Romanov Lane 4
Krylatskoe

www.bloomberg.com
www.murrayolaoire.com

The design of the office reflects the professionalism and modernity of Bloomberg Television. Its interior is made light, bright, and friendly by its minimalist design, stylish furniture, and colorful accents. The multi-media character of the office is underscored by the graphic decoration on the walls.

Das Design des Büros reflektiert die Sachlichkeit und Modernität von Bloomberg Television. Die Interieurs sind leicht, hell und freundlich dank des minimalistischen Designs mit stilvollen Möbeln und farbigen Akzenten. Den medialen Charakter des Büros betont die grafische Gestaltung der Wände.

La conception du bureau reflète l'objectivité et la modernité de Bloomberg Television. Les intérieurs sont légers, clairs et sympathiques grâce à un design minimaliste avec des meubles stylisés et des touches de couleurs. La configuration graphique des murs souligne la fonction médiatique du bureau.

El diseño de la oficina refleja la objetividad y modernidad de Bloomberg Television. Los interiores son ligeros, gratos y claros gracias al diseño minimalista, muebles cargados de estilo y toques de colorido. El carácter mediático de la oficina acentúa la concepción gráfica de las paredes.

Microsoft Headquarters

Murray O'Laoire Architects

2005
Krylatskaya Street 17, Block 1
Krylatskoe

www.microsoft.ru
www.murrayolaoire.com

The primary features of Microsoft buildings are their windows. The same is true for the design of their Moscow office. The fenestration provides air and light and gives the interior an aura of light-hearted comfort. In contrast to the "cold" world of new technologies, the interiors with their bright wooden walls appear warm and friendly.

Das wichtigste bei Microsoft-Gebäuden sind Fenster, so auch bei der Gestaltung des Moskauer Büros. Sie sorgen für Luft und Licht und vermitteln dem Interieur Leichtigkeit. Im Kontrast zur „kalten" Welt der neuen Technologien wirken die Interieurs mit hellen Holzwänden warm und freundlich.

Les fenêtres sont l'élément le plus important des bâtiments de Microsoft; il en va de même pour la réalisation du bureau moscovite. Celles-ci aèrent et éclairent l'espace et lui confèrent sa légèreté. A l'opposé du monde « froid » des nouvelles technologies, les intérieurs paraissent chauds et accueillants grâce aux murs de bois clair.

Lo primordial en los edificios de Microsoft son las ventanas, y así ocurre en el diseño de su oficina de Moscú. Éstas confieren luz y aire transmitiendo a la vez al interior la sensación de ligereza. Frente a la "frialdad" del mundo de las nuevas tecnologías, aquí los interiores con paredes claras de madera emanan calidez y simpatía.

Mercedes Benz Plaza

ABD Architects Ltd., B. Levjant, B. Stuchebrjukov, A. Feoktistova, O. Grouzdev

2004
Leningradsky Prospect 39
North-West District

www.mb-asr.com
www.abdcom.ru

A breath-taking atrium connects the two parts of this building: the long, flat foundation of the showroom and the oval office tower. The high-tech architecture truly does justice to the image of the brand—even though its silhouette rather resembles an enormous submarine.

Ein atemberaubendes Atrium verbindet die zwei Teile dieses Gebäudes, den langen flachen Sockel des Showrooms und den ovalen Büroturm. Die Hightech-Architektur des Hauses entspricht am besten dem Image der Marke – obwohl seine Silhouette eher einem riesigen U-Boot ähnelt.

Un atrium impressionnant relie les deux parties du bâtiment, un long socle plat du showroom et une tour de bureaux ovale. L'architecture haute technologie de l'immeuble correspond à merveille à l'image de la marque – bien que sa silhouette ressemble plutôt à un sous-marin géant.

Un impresionante patio une ambas partes del edificio, el zócalo largo y plano de la sala de exposición y la torre de oficinas oval. La arquitectura de alta tecnología de la casa representa a la perfección la imagen de la marca, pero aquí con una silueta que parece un enorme submarino.

ECN

Arch4, A. Kozyr
A. Plotnikov (SE)

2001
Rochdelskaya Street 8
Presnya

www.arch4.ru

Geometry and light, as well as the open supporting framework and the texture of the materials, play an important role in the design of this office. The materials alone present the nuances of the range from black to white—from the bright glass to the polished black concrete that looks like fine granite.

Geometrie, Licht, sowie das offene Tragwerk und die Textur der Materialien spielen eine wichtige Rolle bei der Gestaltung dieses Büros. Allein durch die Materialien werden hier die Nuancen der Schwarz-Weiß-Palette präsentiert – vom hellen Glas bis zum polierten schwarzen Beton, der wie edler Granit wirkt.

La géométrie, la lumière ainsi que la structure porteuse ouverte et la texture des matériaux jouent un rôle important dans la réalisation de ce bureau. A eux seuls, les matériaux présentent toutes les nuances de la palette noir-blanc – du verre clair au béton poli noir qui ressemble à un superbe granit.

En el diseño de esta oficina la luz, la estructura portante abierta y la textura de los materiales juegan un papel fundamental. Ya los materiales por sí mismos expresan los matices de la gama blanco y negro, desde el vidrio claro, hasta el hormigón negro pulido con efecto de noble granito.

Krylatskiy Hills

ABD Architects Ltd., B. Levjant, B. Stuchebrjukov, I. Mukosey
SWA (USA) (Landscape Architecture)

2006
Krylatskaya Street 19
Krylatskoe

www.abdcom.ru

A concave complex of five modern office buildings surrounds a tranquil hill, blending into the picturesque banks of the Moskva. The metal-glass façade provides high transparency—in and out.

Ein konkaver Komplex aus fünf modernen Bürohäusern umrahmt einen sanften Hügel und fügt sich in die malerische Uferlandschaft der Moskva ein. Die Metall- und Glasfassade bietet hohe Transparenz – von innen und von außen.

Un complexe concave de cinq immeubles de bureaux modernes entoure une petite colline et s'intègre parfaitement dans le paysage pittoresque des bords de la Moskova. La façade de verre et d'acier assure une transparence maximale – de l'intérieur comme de l'extérieur.

Un complejo cóncavo compuesto por cinco modernos edificios de oficinas rodea una ligera colina integrándose en el pintoresco paisaje de las orillas del Moscova. La fachada de metal y vidrio ofrece una alta transparencia tanto desde el interior como desde el exterior.

Exhibition Center Manege
Reconstruction

Mosprojekt 2, A. Kuzmin, M. Posokhin, P. Andreev, S. Pavlov, O. Galanitcheva
B. Shafran, S. Turovskiy (SE)

2005
Manezhnaya Place 1
Center

Built in 1817, this hall served as an exhibition center for decades. It took on a new shape following its reconstruction after a catastrophic fire in 2004; prominence was given to the contrast between old and new. The buoyant conference room and the upper gallery seem like design objects.

Die nach dem verheerenden Brand im Jahr 2004 wiederhergestellte Halle von 1817, die seit Jahrzehnten als Ausstellungshalle diente, bekam eine neue Gestalt. Der Kontrast zwischen Altem und Neuen wurde betont. Der schwungvolle Konferenzraum und die obere Galerie sehen aus wie Designobjekte.

Cette halle datant de 1817 et reconstruite après l'incendie dévastateur de 2004, servait depuis des décennies de halle d'expositions. Elle a été remodelée et le contraste entre l'ancien et le nouveau a été souligné. La salle de conférences, toute en courbes, et la galerie supérieure ressemblent à des objets design.

El pabellón de 1817, reconstruido tras el devastador incendio de 2004 y que desde hace décadas ha servido como sala de exposiciones ha adoptado una nueva forma. En ella se ha puesto de relieve el contraste entre lo antiguo y lo moderno. La dinámica sala de conferencias y la galería superior parecen verdaderos objetos de diseño.

Romanov Cinema

Lab for Virtual Architecture, S. Kulish, V. Lipatov (Interior Design)
Yu. Ponamarev (SE)

2004
Romanov Lane 4
Center

www.romanov-cinema.ru
www.labva.ru

Audiences are greeted by a magical world right in the vestibule of this movie theater. It is a place of perfect interaction—the twinkling, mostly transparent materials reflect colors and light that glow from above and below, blurring the line between illusion and reality.

Eine zauberhafte Welt erwartet die Zuschauer bereits im Vestibül des Kinos. Hier fließt alles ineinander – die glitzernden, meist transparenten Materialien reflektieren Farben und Licht, die von unten und oben strahlen, und verwischen die Grenzen zwischen illusorischer und realer Welt.

Un monde enchanteur attend le spectateur dès le vestibule du cinéma. Ici, tout se fond et se confond – les matériaux scintillants, le plus souvent transparents, reflètent les couleurs et la lumière qui irradient de toutes parts et estompent les frontières entre réalité et illusion.

Ya en el vestíbulo del cine se abre a los espectadores un mundo de fantasía. Allí se funden materiales brillantes, la mayoría transparentes, reflejando colores y luz emitida desde abajo y desde arriba que difuminan las fronteras entre ilusión y realidad.

Culture Center Tipografia

Meganom, A. Kurennoy, Yurj Grigoryan, Alexandra Pavlova, Pavel Ivantchikov, Ilja Kuleshov, V. Soshnikov
M. Kelman (SE)

2000
Bol. Putinkovsky Lane 5-7
Center

Built in 1909, the "Utro Rossii" print shop was carefully restored and converted into a cultural center with an antique shop, club, restaurant, and offices. The building now has a glass cube with panoramic elevators and a courtyard serving as a public area.

Die im Jahre 1909 erbaute Druckerei „Utro Rossii" wurde sorgsam saniert und zum Kulturzentrum mit Antiquitätenladen, Club, Restaurant und Büros umgebaut. Das Gebäude hat nun einen gläsernen Kubus mit Panorama-Fahrstühlen und einen Hof, der als öffentlicher Raum dient.

L'imprimerie « Utro Rossii », construite en 1909, a été réhabilitée avec soin et transformée en centre culturel avec magasin d'antiquités, club, restaurant et bureaux. Le bâtiment comprend à présent un cube de verre avec des ascenseurs panoramiques et une cour qui sert d'espace public.

La imprenta "Utro Rossii", fundada en 1909, ha sido saneada cuidadosamente para convertirse en un centro cultural con comercios de antigüedades, club, restaurante y oficinas. El edificio cuenta ahora con un cubo de vidrio con ascensores panorámicos, además de un patio que hace las funciones de salón abierto.

Kino Gallery

Arch4, N. Lobanova, I. Perminov

2003
Bol. Rzhevsky Lane 8
Arbat

www.gallerykino.ru
www.arch4.ru

The name of this art gallery stems from its former accommodation in a cinema center. Indeed, the gallery seems to have a cinematographic aura. Maybe it's the white row of seats along the walls—or the magical appearance of the light boxes made of multi-colored glass.

Ihre frühere Unterbringung in einem Kinozentrum gab dieser Kunstgalerie ihren Namen. Sie wirkt auch etwas kinematographisch. Vielleicht kommt es von der weiß lackierten Sitzreihe entlang der Wände oder von den magisch wirkenden Leuchtkästen aus buntem Glas.

Cette galerie d'art doit son nom au fait qu'elle était antérieurement logée dans un complexe de cinémas. D'ailleurs, elle a un peu une apparence cinématographique. Cela vient peut-être de la rangée de sièges laqués de blanc, le long du mur, ou des caissons de lumière, en verre coloré, aux effets magiques.

La galería debe su nombre al hecho de que en el pasado estaba ubicada en un edificio de multicines; y a decir verdad tiene un aire cinematográfico que tal vez se debe a las filas de sillas lacadas en blanco situadas a lo largo de las paredes o bien a los cajones luminosos de vidrio multicolor de efecto casi mágico.

Ru Arts Gallery

Atrium, A. Nadtochy, V. Butko, O. Sokolova, A. Malygin
L. Bujanova, O. Pichugina (SE)

2004
1. Zachatjevskij Lane 10
Ostozhenka

www.ruarts.ru
www.atrium.ru

The most important space-shaping aspect of this gallery is the staircase linking the four levels. These stairs form elements that are tilted off their axis, around which all rooms concentrate. They actually seem like sculptures that communicate with each other and create numerous optical effects.

Die wichtigsten Raum schaffenden Elemente dieser Galerie sind die Treppen, die vier Ebenen verbinden. Sie bilden um die Achse gekippte Elemente, um die sich alle Räume konzentrieren, und wirken selbst wie Skulpturen, die miteinander kommunizieren und zahlreiche optische Effekte schaffen.

Les véritables éléments créateurs d'espace dans cette galerie sont les escaliers qui relient quatre niveaux. Ce sont des éléments basculant sur leur axe autour desquels se concentrent toutes les pièces et ils font eux-mêmes figure de sculptures qui communiquent entre elles et créent de nombreux effets d'optique.

Los elementos fundamentales que dotan de espacio a la galería son las escaleras que vinculan los cuatro niveles. Éstas crean elementos volcados en su eje en torno a los cuales se concentran todas las salas, y asemejan a esculturas comunicadas entre sí desprendiendo innumerables efectos ópticos.

National Centre for Contemporary Arts

M. Khazanov Studio, M. Mindlin, N. Shangin, M. Rebrova, M. Khazanov
A. Timofeevich, M. Mitiukov, N. Kancheli (SE)

2004
Zoologicheskaya Street 13
Presnya

www.ncca.ru

The former factory site for theater and stage materials has been restored and converted into a sophisticated museum center. Its industrial character has been preserved and strongly highlighted by the construction on its façades and by the external red stairwell tower.

Die ehemalige Fabrikationsstätte für Theater- und Bühnenbedarf wurde saniert und zu einem modernen Museumszentrum umgebaut. Den industriellen Charakter hat man dabei erhalten und durch die an den Fassaden ausgetragenen Konstruktionen und den externen roten Treppenturm stark betont.

L'ancien atelier de fabrication d'accessoires de théâtre et de scène a été réhabilité et transformé en un musée moderne. On lui a conservé son caractère industriel, très bien souligné par les constructions rapportées sur les façades et la cage d'escalier extérieure rouge.

La antigua fábrica para material de teatro y de escenario ha sido saneada y transformada en un moderno museo. El carácter industrial se ha mantenido e incluso se ha acentuado más gracias a las construcciones aplicadas a las fachadas y a la torre de escaleras externa de color rojo.

Yakut Gallery at Gasholder

Alexander Yakut

2005
Nizhny Sussalniy Lane 5
Kurskaja

www.yakutgallery.ru

If you're up to an adventurous search for an old industrial park behind Kursk Station, you'll be richly rewarded. One of three former brick gasholders houses a gallery for contemporary art run by the architect and gallery owner Alexander Yakut.

Wer auf die abenteuerliche Suche nach einem alten Industriegebiet hinter dem Kursker Bahnhof nicht verzichtet, wird reich belohnt. In einem von drei ehemaligen Backsteingasometern befindet sich eine Galerie für zeitgenössische Kunst, die der Architekt und Galerist Alexander Yakut betreibt.

Celui qui voudra s'aventurer à la recherche d'un ancien quartier industriel derrière la gare de Koursk, sera largement récompensé. Dans un complexe constitué de trois anciens gazomètres en briques se trouve une galerie consacrée à l'art contemporain et gérée par l'architecte et galeriste Alexander Yakut.

Quien no quiera renunciar a la aventurera búsqueda de una antigua zona industrial detrás de la estación Kursk será recompensado. En uno de los tres antiguos gasómetros de ladrillo se ubica una galería de arte contemporáneo dirigida por el arquitecto y galerista Alexander Yakut.

School for Autistic Children

A. A. Chernikhov' Design and Architecture Studio, A. A. Chernikhov
M. Karmin (SE)

2001
Kashenkin Lug 7
Ostankino

The school's architecture supports the work of psychologists and educators. Geometrical archetypes like the circle, triangle, square or spiral, and rhythmic repetitions or asymmetry create the feel of a geometrical ABC. This is not just supposed to appeal to the children's senses, but also their unconscious.

Durch die Architektur des Komplexes wird die Arbeit der Psychologen und Erzieher unterstützt. Geometrische Archetypen wie Kreis, Dreieck, Viereck oder Spirale sowie rhythmische Wiederholungen und Asymmetrie schaffen das Gefühl eines geometrischen ABC, das nicht nur die Sinne, sondern auch das Unterbewusstsein der Kinder ansprechen soll.

L'architecture du complexe vient appuyer le travail des psychologues et des éducateurs. Des archétypes géométriques tels que le cercle, le triangle, le quadrilatère ou la spirale ainsi que des répétitions rythmiques et une asymétrie donnent l'impression d'un ABC géométrique qui n'interpelle pas seulement les sens mais aussi l'inconscient des enfants.

La arquitectura del complejo cumple una función de apoyo al trabajo de los psicólogos y educadores. Una serie de arquetipos geométricos como el círculo, el triángulo y el cuadrado o la espiral, así como las repeticiones rítmicas y asimetrías crean la sensación de un abecedario geométrico destinado a estimular no sólo los sentidos sino al mismo tiempo el subconsciente de los niños.

Residential School for Orphans

Atrium, A. Nadtochy, V. Butko, V. Gurchev, A. Shapiro, V. Shlaykov,
S. Haritonova, E. Valuyskih
A. Kalashnikov (SE)

2006
1. Kraskovsky Lane 386
Kozhuhovo

www.atrium.ru

This boarding school for 110 children was planned as a complex of four two- and three-story buildings. Two dormitories, the school, and the gymnasium are linked by a gallery on the first floor. Light, organic shapes, as well as joyous, bright colors give the complex a playfully natural character.

Das Internat für 110 Kinder wurde als Komplex aus vier zwei- bis dreistöckigen Gebäuden geplant. Zwei Wohnhäuser, Schule und Sporthalle sind durch eine Galerie im ersten Stock verbunden. Leichte, organische Formen, sowie fröhliche, helle Farben geben dem Ganzen einen verspielt ungezwungenen Charakter.

Les plans de cet internat pour 110 enfants ont prévu un complexe de quatre bâtiments de deux à trois étages. Deux résidences, une école et un gymnase sont reliés par une galerie au premier étage. Des formes légères et organiques, des couleurs gaies et claires confèrent à l'ensemble un caractère espiègle et détendu.

Este internado para 110 niños fue planeado como complejo de cuatro edificios de dos a tres plantas. Los dos edificios de viviendas, el colegio y el pabellón de deportes se unen a través de una galería por el primer piso. Las formas ligeras y orgánicas, acompañadas de colores alegres y claros transmiten al lugar un carácter lúdico y desenfadado.

Entertaining Center Ibiza

A. Asadov, N. Tsymbal, A. A. Asadov, S. Terehov, M. Shvan, G. Shitova
D. Matrovsov (SE)

2005
Stroginskoe Chausse 33
Strogino

www.contigroup.ru
www.asadov.ru

This building's purpose and proximity to the river has impacted its design. The structure—containing a casino, billiard room, bars, cafés, and a dance club—has slanted façades, large glass surfaces, and cheerful colors that make it seem to float like a huge, multi-colored sail.

Die Funktion des Gebäudes und seine Nähe zum Fluss haben die Gestaltung beeinflusst. Ein Haus mit Spielkasino, Billardsaal, Bars, Cafés und Disko sieht dank der geneigten Fassaden, großen Glasflächen und fröhlichen Farben leicht, fast schwebend aus – wie ein großes, buntes Segel.

La fonction de ce bâtiment et sa situation à proximité de la rivière ont influencé sa conception. Une maison avec casino, salle de billard, bars, cafés et discothèque qui, grâce à ses façades inclinées, aux larges surfaces de verre et aux couleurs gaies, paraît légère, planant presque – comme une grande voile colorée.

La función del edificio y su cercanía al río han influido claramente en su concepción. La construcción con casino, sala de billar, bares, cafeterías y discoteca con grandes superficies acristaladas y colores vivos se levanta casi flotante como una enorme vela.

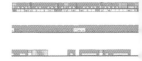

Mercury Theater

Meganom, Yurj Grigoryan, Alexandra Pavlova, Pavel Ivantchikov, Ilja Kuleshov

2006
Barvicha Village

At the end of this luxury village, a theater for 800 people is under construction. Its complex shape contrasts with the wooden cubes of nearby high-end boutiques. The vertical wood slats of different contours make its façades appear as if they are in constant motion.

Am Ende des Luxusdorfes entsteht ein Theater für 800 Zuschauer. Seine komplexe Form kontrastiert mit den hölzernen Kuben von Luxusboutiquen. Die vertikalen Holzlamellen unterschiedlicher Konturen lassen seine Fassaden so wirken, als befänden sie sich in ständiger Bewegung.

A la sortie du village de luxe se construit un théâtre pour 800 spectateurs. Sa forme sophistiquée contraste avec les cubes de bois des boutiques de luxe. Les lamelles de bois verticales aux contours variés donnent l'impression que les façades sont en perpétuel mouvement.

Al final de este poblado de lujo se levanta un teatro con cabida para 800 espectadores. Su compleja forma contrasta con los cubos de madera de las boutiques de lujo. Las láminas verticales de madera de diferentes conturas hacen que la fachada parezca estar en continuo movimiento.

Our Artists Gallery

Asse Architects, E. Asse, L. Tulupova, V. Arutyunyan

2004
Rublevo-Uspenskoe Chausse
Barchiva Village

www.kournikovagallery.ru

The outside of this modern building suggests that it consists of two parts. The interior, however, tells a different story. This old residential building was rebuilt and its original tripartite room structure was retained. Thanks to a stylish and functional conversion, the building serves its new purpose as a gallery perfectly.

Das moderne Haus besteht optisch aus zwei Volumina, was jedoch seiner inneren Struktur nicht entspricht. Man hat das alte Wohnhaus umgebaut und dabei die dreiteilige Raumstruktur beibehalten. Doch dank der stilvollen und funktionalen Neugestaltung entspricht das Haus seinen neuen Anforderungen als Galerie optimal.

Cette maison moderne est constituée optiquement de deux volumes, ce qui, pourtant, ne correspond pas à sa structure intérieure. On a transformé la vieille maison d'habitation en conservant la division de l'espace en trois parties. Mais grâce à une recomposition stylisée et fonctionnelle, la maison répond parfaitement aux nouvelles exigences de sa fonction, celles d'une galerie.

La moderna construcción está compuesta ópticamente por dos volúmenes, que sin embargo no corresponden a su estructura interior. La antigua vivienda ha sido remodelada conservando una estructura espacial de tres partes. Pero gracias a un nuevo diseño cargado de estilo y funcionalidad la casa refleja a la perfección las nuevas exigencias de una galería.

Metro Majakovskaya

N. Shumakov, G. Mun, Ja. Mun
I.Lubennikov (Mosaic)
M. Belova, E. Hanukova, D. Saveljeva (SE)

2005
Zamoskvoretskaya Line
Center

www.arhmetro.ru

One of the most beautiful stations of the Moscow Metro subway has been provided with a second exit to Tverskaya Street. The golden mosaic ceiling of the new vestibule bears clouds and quotations from a famous poet of the revolution, for whom the station was named.

Eine der schönsten Stationen der Moskauer Metro bekam einen zweiten Ausgang zur Tverskaya-Straße. Auf dem goldenen Mosaikplafond des neuen Vestibüls fliegen die Wolken und Zitate aus den Gedichten des berühmten Dichters der Revolution, dessen Namen die Station trägt.

Une des plus belles stations du métro de Moscou où une deuxième sortie sur la rue Tverskaya a été construite. Sur la mosaïque dorée du plafond du nouveau hall flottent des nuages et des citations des poèmes du célèbre poète de la révolution dont la station porte le nom.

En una de las estaciones de metro más atractivas de Moscú se ha abierto una segunda salida a la calle Tverskaya. Sobre el techo dorado de mosaico del nuevo vestíbulo se dibujan nubes y citas de poemas de los poetas de la revolución, que dan nombre a la estación.

Federation Tower

Peter Schweger, ASP Schweger Assoziierte Gesamtplanung GmbH
Sergei Tchoban, nps tchoban voss Architekten BDA
TTG Thornton Tomasetti Group, New York (SE)

2008
Krasnopresnenskaya Naberezhnaya,
Parcel No. 13
MIBC Moscow City

www.schweger-architekten.eu
www.nps-tchoban-voss.de

Reaching 1,480 feet with its antenna, this complex consists of two glass towers that rise from a joint foundation and group themselves around a slim mast. Panoramic elevators take visitors to the public viewing platform underneath the cupola of the taller tower to enjoy a spectacular view of the city.

Der mit Antenne 450 m hohe Komplex besteht aus zwei gläsernen Türmen, die aus einem gemeinsamen Sockel wachsen und sich um einen schlanken Mast gruppieren. Mit Panorama-Aufzügen erreicht man die öffentliche Aussichtsplattform unter der Kuppel des höheren Turms und kann einen einzigartigen Ausblick über die Stadt genießen.

Le complexe d'une hauteur de 450 m, antenne comprise, se compose de deux tours de verre jaillissant d'un socle commun et disposées autour d'un mât élancé. Par des ascenseurs panoramiques, on accède à la plate-forme d'observation destinée au public, sous la coupole de la plus haute tour, d'où l'on bénéficie d'une vue extraordinaire sur la ville.

El complejo dotado de antenas de 450 m está formado por dos torres de vidrio que brotan de un único zócalo y se agrupan en torno a un estrecho mástil. A través de ascensores panorámicos se accede a la plataforma pública situada bajo la cúpula de la torre más alta, desde donde se pueden disfrutar las magníficas vistas sobre la ciudad.

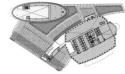

Moscow International Business Center

Swanke Hayden Connell Architects, Altan O. Gursel, Roger Klein
L. Zborovsky, TTG Thornton Tomasetti Group, New York (Summa Construction)

2007
Krasnopresnenskaya Naberezhnaya,
Parcel No. 12
MIBC Moscow City

www.shca.com

This mixed-use 78 story tower on a 2.5 acre site in central Moscow houses 50 floors of office space, and 20 floors atop containing luxury residential apartments with gymnasium and swimming pool. It rises out of a retail and entertainment podium that includes boutiques, restaurants, bars, a hotel, and a 32,000 sq ft casino.

Dieser multifunktionale 78-stöckige Turm auf einem 1,4 ha großen Grundstück im Zentrum Moskaus beherbergt 50 Stockwerke mit Büros und darüber weitere 20 mit Luxuswohnungen, die mit Fitnessclub und Schwimmbad ausgestattet sind. Der Turm erhebt sich aus einem Einkaufs- und Vergnügungszentrum, in dem sich Boutiquen, Restaurants, Bars, ein Hotel und ein 3000 m² großes Kasino befinden.

Cette tour multifonctions de 78 étages sur 1,4 hectare au centre de Moscou abrite 50 étages de bureaux, les 20 étages supérieurs étant occupés par des appartements résidentiels de luxe avec gymnase et piscine. Elle surgit d'un socle destiné au commerce et aux loisirs comprenant magasins, restaurants, bars, un hôtel et un casino d'env. 3000 m².

Esta torre multifuncional de 78 plantas erigida en un recinto de 1,4 hectárea está ubicada en el centro de Moscú y alberga 50 pisos de oficinas y, sobre ellos, otros 20 con apartamentos de lujo que incluyen un gimnasio y piscina. La torre se levanta por encima de un centro comercial y de ocio, dotado además de boutiques, restaurantes, bares, un hotel y un casino de 3000 m².

Moscow City Tower

Foster and Partners, Mosprojekt 2
Halvorson and Partners (USA) (SE)

2009
Krasnopresnenskaya Naberezhnaya
Parcel No. 17-18
MIBC Moscow City

www.fosterandpartners.com

This tower, measuring 1,970 feet, is to become the tallest building with natural ventilation. Despite its enormous height, the tower will have a light and dynamic appearance composed of three glass prisms tapering towards the top and grouping themselves around the communication core.

Ein 600 m hoher Turm soll das höchste Gebäude mit natürlicher Belüftung werden. Trotz der gewaltigen Höhe bekommt das Haus eine leichte und dynamische Erscheinung dank seiner Komposition aus drei gläsernen Prismen, die sich nach oben verjüngen und sich um den Kommunikationskern gruppieren.

La plus haute construction avec une aération naturelle sera une tour de 600 m de haut. Malgré cette hauteur imposante, le bâtiment paraît léger et dynamique de par sa conception basée sur trois prismes de verre qui s'articulent autour du noyau de communication et se rétrécissent vers le haut.

La torre de 600 m será el edificio con ventilación natural más elevado. A pesar de la imponente altura la casa se muestra dinámica, gracias a su composición de tres prismas de vidrio que se estrechan hacia lo alto agrupándose en torno al centro de comunicación.

Metro Delovoy Center

L. Borzenkov, A. Vigdorov, A. Farstova

2005
Fili Line
MIBC Moscow City

www.arhmetro.ru

This station is the first of the "mini line" connecting the International Business Center Moscow City with the center of the city and the Metro network. The primary principles of Moscow City's design—clear lines along with modern shapes and materials—have been implemented underground as well.

Diese Station ist die erste der „Mini-Linie", die das internationale Geschäftszentrum Moscow City mit dem Zentrum der Stadt und dem Metronetz verbindet. Die wichtigsten Gestaltungsprinzipien der Moscow City wurden auch unterirdisch umgesetzt – klare Linien sowie moderne Formen und Materialien.

Cette station est la première d' la « mini ligne » qui relie le centr international des affaires Mos cow City avec le centre de l ville et le réseau métropolitain Les plus importants principes d conception de Moscow City on également été réalisés sou terre – des lignes droites ains que des formes et des matériau modernes.

Esta estación es la primera "mini línea" de metro que enlaza el centro internacional de negocios Moscow City con el centro de la ciudad. Los principios de diseño fundamentales de Moscow City han sido también aplicados bajo tierra: líneas claras y materiales y formas modernas.

Garage

Lyzlov's Architectural Studio, N. Lyzlov, O. Kaverina, A. Krasnov
E. Shabalin (SE)

2002
9. Parkovaya Street 60-62
Izmailovo

www.lyzlov.ru

Statics and dynamics, openness and reserve, transparency and materiality, functionality and aesthetics—it's hard to believe that the design of a simple garage cube can unite so many perpetual architectural challenges and find individual formal solutions for all of them.

Statik und Dynamik, Offenheit und Verschlossenheit, Transparenz und Materialität, Funktionalität und Ästhetik – kaum zu glauben, dass sich in der Gestaltung eines einfachen Garagenkubus so viele ewige Architekturfragen vereinen lassen und für alle eigene formale Lösungen angeboten werden.

Statique et dynamique, ouverture et fermeture, transparence et matérialité, fonctionnalité et esthétique – incroyable de constater que la conception d'un simple parking en forme de cube réunisse tant de questions éternelles en matière d'architecture et que soient proposées pour chacune d'elles des solutions formelles individuelles.

Estática y dinámica, apertura y hermetismo, transparencia y materialidad, funcionalidad y estética. Parece mentira que la concepción de un simple cubo garaje encierre tantas y tan eternas cuestiones arquitectónicas, y ofrezca una solución formal para cada una de ellas.

Metro Vorobyovi Gori

N. Shumakov, L. Borzenkov, A. Vigdorov
G. Petrov, N. Korneeva, E. Meleshonkova (SE)

2002
Sokolnizcheskaya Line
University

www.arhmetro.ru

This station was constructed on a bridge. It offers a fantastic view of the green hills, the river, and the magnitude of the city. The lightness and the panoramic glazing of the old station have been preserved and highlighted with shining modern materials.

Diese Station wurde auf einer Brücke gebaut. Von hier aus kann man den herrlichen Blick auf die grünen Hügel, den Fluss und die Weite der Stadt genießen. Die Leichtigkeit und Panorama-Verglasung der alten Station wurden erhalten und durch die glänzenden modernen Materialien betont.

Cette station a été construite su un pont. De là, on a une vue ma gnifique sur les collines ver doyantes, la rivière et l'étendu de la ville. La légèreté et le vi trage panoramique de l'ancienn station ont été conservés et mi en valeur par des matériaux mo dernes brillants.

La construcción fue erigida sobre un puente. Desde aquí se divisa la fantástica vista a las verdes colinas, el río y la inmensidad de la ciudad. La ligereza y acristalamiento panorámico de la antigua estación se han mantenido y acentuado con brillantes materiales modernos.

Metro Butovo

L. Borzenkov, A. Vigdorov, N. Shumakov
O. Krasnov, D. Labuzov, A. Korkin (SE)

2003
Butovskaya Line
Butovo

www.arhmetro.ru

The new, 1.2-mile Metro line in the north of the city has offered solutions for many problems. Located above ground, it makes allowances for the regular road network, it was easy and cost-effective to build, and—above all—its open construction is quite handsome and doesn't need decoration.

Die neue, 2 km lange Metrolinie im Norden der Stadt hat Lösungen für viele Probleme gefunden. Sie liegt oberirdisch und berücksichtigt das gewöhnliche Straßennetz, sie war leicht und günstig zu errichten und vor allem ist ihre offene Konstruktion wirklich schön und braucht keine Dekoration.

La nouvelle ligne de métro de 2 km de long, au nord de la ville, apporte des solutions à de nombreux problèmes. Aérienne, elle prend en compte le réseau routier existant ; elle a été construite facilement et économiquement. Et surtout, sa construction ouverte est vraiment belle et ne nécessite aucune décoration.

La nueva línea de metro de 2 km que transcurre por el norte de la ciudad ha conseguido encontrar soluciones a numerosos problemas. Está construida sobre la tierra teniendo en cuenta la red de carreteras habitual. Fue además de construcción fácil y económica y, lo más importante, su estructura abierta es estética en sí misma y no requiere ningún tipo de decoración.

to stay . hotels

105

Ararat Park Hyatt Moscow

Yevgeny Serov, Sarkis Gurdzanyan, Victor Krasnikiov, Mikhail Shishkov

2002
Neglinnaya Street 4
Tverskoe

www.moscow.park.hyatt.com

A luxury hotel right in the heart of the city offers its guests elegance, modernity, and exclusivity. Its attractions include an atrium and a restaurant on the roof terrace providing a spectacular view of the Kremlin and the Red Square.

Ein Luxushotel ganz im Herzen der Stadt bietet seinen Gästen Eleganz, Modernität und Exklusivität an. Die Hauptanziehungspunkte sind sein Atrium und ein Restaurant auf der Dachterrasse, von wo man den einzigartigen Blick auf den Kreml und den Roten Platz genießen kann.

Cet hôtel de luxe situé au cœur de la ville offre à ses hôtes élégance, modernité et exclusivité. Ses pôles d'attraction principaux sont l'atrium et un restaurant en terrasse sur le toit, d'où l'on jouit d'une vue unique sur le Kremlin et la Place Rouge.

Un hotel de lujo en el corazón de la ciudad que ofrece a sus huéspedes elegancia, modernidad y exclusividad. Los principales puntos de atracción son el atrio y el restaurante sobre el ático, desde donde se puede disfrutar de una inigualable vista al Kremlin y la Plaza Roja.

Golden Apple Boutique Hotel

Rafael Shafir, Zebra Crossing Design

2004
Malaya Dmitrovka 11
Center

www.goldenapple.ru

This building from the late 19th century today houses the Moscow's first boutique hotel. Its minimalist design is based on the contrast of the materials, light effects, and colorful accents. Each of its six stories has its own color while all 92 rooms of the four categories come with the same decoration.

In einem Haus vom Ende des 19. Jahrhunderts ist heute das erste Moskauer Boutique-Hotel untergebracht. Sein minimalistisches Design basiert auf dem Kontrast der Materialien, Lichtspielen und farblichen Akzente. Jede seiner sechs Etagen hat eine eigene Farbe, aber alle 92 Zimmer der vier Kategorien haben die gleiche Ausstattung.

Le premier hôtel boutique de Moscou est aujourd'hui abrité dans un immeuble datant de la fin du 19ème siècle. Son design minimaliste repose sur le contraste entre les matériaux, les jeux de lumière et les touches de couleur. Chacun des six étages est caractérisé par sa propre couleur mais toutes les 92 chambres des quatre catégories possèdent le même aménagement.

En una casa de finales del siglo XIX hoy se ubica el primer hotel boutique de Moscú. El diseño minimalista se basa en los contrastes entre materiales, juegos de luz y toques de color. Cada una de sus seis plantas tiene un color diferente, pero las 92 habitaciones de las cuatro categorías cuentan con la misma decoración.

Metropol

William Walcott

1901
Teatralniy Lane 1/4
Center

www.metropol-moscow.ru

This famous, long-established house was founded by Savva Mamontov in 1901 and decorated by the best Russian artists: M. Vrubel, V. Vasnetsov, and S. Chehonin. Although the hotel has been renovated and redecorated several times since, it has always remained the same luxurious Metropol.

Das berühmte, traditionsreiche Haus wurde im Jahr 1901 von Savva Mamontov gegründet und von den besten russischen Künstlern M. Vrubel, V. Vasnetsov, S. Chehonin ausgestattet. Seit dieser Zeit ist das Hotel mehrmals renoviert und umgebaut worden, aber immer dasselbe, luxuriöse Metropol geblieben.

Cet établissement célèbre et porteur de traditions a été fondé en 1901 par Savva Mamontov et aménagé par les meilleurs artistes russes, M. Vrubel, V. Vasnetsov, S. Chehonin. L'hôtel a, depuis, été rénové et transformé à de nombreuses reprises mais il est toujours resté le même luxueux Metropol.

La famosa y tradicional casa fue fundada en el año 1901 por Savva Mamontov y decorada por los mejores artistas rusos, M. Vrubel, V. Vasnetsov y S. Chehonin. Desde entonces el hotel ha sido renovado y transformado en diversas ocasiones manteniéndose siempre como metrópoli del lujo.

Le Royal Meridien National

Alexander Ivanov

built 1903, renovated in 1995
Mokhovaya Street 15/1
Tverskoe

www.national.ru

This traditional house with its more than 100-year-old history is located in the heart of Moscow, facing the Kremlin. Time after time, its facilities have been modernized without sacrificing the charm of an older era. It is made especially attractive by its good location.

Im Herzen Moskaus mit Blick auf den Kreml steht das traditionelle Haus mit einer über 100-jährigen Geschichte. Nach und nach wurden in den letzten Jahren Räumlichkeiten modernisiert ohne den Charme einer alten Ära zu verlieren. Die gute Lage macht es besonders attraktiv.

Au cœur de Moscou, avec vue sur le Kremlin, se dresse cet établissement traditionnel, porteur d'un siècle d'histoire. Petit à petit, ces dernières années, les locaux ont été modernisés, sans toutefois perdre le charme de la vieille époque. Très bien situé, il est particulièrement attrayant.

En el corazón de Moscú y con vistas al Kremlin se levanta esta casa tradicional que cuenta con más de 100 años de historia. En los últimos años se han ido modernizando las estancias progresivamente sin que por ello perdieran el encanto de una era pasada. Parte de su atractivo se debe sin duda a la buena situación.

The Hotel Baltschug Kempinski Moscow

Awstroj Baugesellshaft mbh & Co KG

built in 1898, renovated in 1991
Balchug Street 1
Zamoskvoretchye

www.kempinski-moscow.com

This house on the bank of the Moskva across from the Kremlin was built in 1898 and rebuilt several times afterward. Since its last renovation, the hotel has combined the generosity of its historical rooms — as the tradition of the grand hotels dictates — with state-of-the-art convenience.

Das Haus am Ufer der Moskva gegenüber dem Kreml wurde im Jahr 1898 errichtet und später mehrmals umgebaut. Nach seiner letzten Renovierung vereint das Hotel die Großzügigkeit der historischen Räume – ganz in der Tradition der Grand-Hotels – mit modernem Komfort.

L'immeuble sur les rives de la Moskova, en face du Kremlin, a été édifié en 1898 et plusieurs fois transformé au fil des ans. Depuis sa dernière rénovation, l'hôtel propose tout le confort moderne dans de grandes chambres aux dimensions d'origine – dans la pure tradition des Grands Hôtels.

Esta casa a orillas del Moscova y enfrente del Kremlin fue levantada en el año 1898 y posteriormente reestructurada en varias ocasiones. Tras su última renovación el hotel ha conseguido conciliar la generosidad de las estancias históricas, en la tradición de un Grand Hotel, con el confort moderno.

Swissôtel Krasnye Holmy Moscow

BBG-BBGM

2005
Kosmodamianskaya Embankment 52
Bldg. 6
Paveletskaya

www.moscow.swissotel.com
www.bbg-bbgm.com

This modern hotel is located in a round, 34-story tower at the Garden Ring near the Moskva. It offers comfortable, modern, and stylishly decorated rooms, bars, and lounges as well as a breathtaking view of the city center.

Das moderne Hotel befindet sich in einem 34-stöckigen runden Turm am Garten-Ring in der Nähe der Moskva und bietet nicht nur komfortable, modern und stilvoll eingerichtete Zimmer, Bars und Lounges, sondern auch atemberaubende Blicke auf das Zentrum der Stadt.

Cet hôtel moderne, situé dans une tour ronde de 34 étages sur le quai des jardins à proximité de la Moskova, ne propose pas seulement des chambres confortables, modernes et meublées avec goût, des bars et des salons mais aussi une vue spectaculaire sur le centre ville.

Este moderno hotel está ubicado en una torre circular de 34 pisos en torno al muelle con jardines que rodea al Moscova. El hotel ofrece habitaciones con estilo confortables y modernas, bares y lounges, además de una fascinante vista al centro de la ciudad.

to go . eating
drinking
clubbing
wellness, beauty & sport

Biscuit

Albina Nazimova

2001
Kuznetsky Street 19, Bldg. 1
Meshchanskoe

www.novikovgroup.ru

The style of a fine Paris salon from the mid-19th century is perfectly copied in this restaurant; its deep, posh armchairs, oversized mirrors, and sparkling chandeliers send today's high society of Moscow back into the time of Napoleon III. Star chefs from all over the world honor Biscuit on a regular basis.

Der Stil eines feinen Pariser Salons aus der Mitte des 19. Jahrhunderts wird mit tiefen, überladenen Sesseln, übergroßen Spiegeln und funkelnden Lüstern perfekt kopiert und damit die heutige High Society Moskaus in die Zeit Napoleons III. zurückversetzt. Starköche aus aller Welt beehren das Biscuit regelmäßig.

Le style d'un salon parisien raffiné de la seconde moitié du 19ème siècle est parfaitement copié avec ses fauteuils profonds et chargés, ses miroirs surdimensionnés et ses lustres scintillants. Ce qui transporte la haute société moscovite d'aujourd'hui à l'époque de Napoléon III. Des vedettes de la gastronomie du monde entier font régulièrement l'honneur de leurs talents au Biscuit.

Una perfecta copia del estilo de un refinado salón parisino de mediados del siglo XIX, que se envuelve de sillones cargados y profundos, espejos supradimensionales, y lámparas de araña resplandecientes, todo ello con el objeto de trasladar a la actual alta sociedad moscovita a los tiempos de Napoleón III. Grandes cocineros de todo el mundo agasajan regularmente al Biscuit con sus artes culinarias.

122

Vogue Café

Ann Boyd

2003
Kuznetsky Street 7/9
Tverskoe

www.novikovgroup.ru

Whether it's coffee in the afternoon or dinner at night, the Vogue Café has been the insider tip for fashion- and trend-oriented clientele for years. Its ambience is elegant and classic at the same time. Vogue magazine lends not only its name, but also exhibits a large selection of its fashion photography here.

Ob Kaffee am Nachmittag oder Dinner am Abend, das Vogue Café ist seit Jahren der Insidertipp für ein mode- und trendbewusstes Publikum. Das Ambiente ist elegant und zugleich klassisch. Die Zeitschrift Vogue stellt nicht nur den Namen, sondern auch eine große Auswahl ihrer Modefotografien, die hier ausgestellt sind.

Que ce soit pour un café l'après-midi ou un dîner en soirée, le Vogue Café est, depuis des années, une adresse d'initiés pour un public attentif à la mode et aux tendances. L'atmosphère y est élégante et classique à la fois. Le magazine Vogue lui prête son nom et y expose également une large sélection de ses photos de mode.

Ya sea para un café por la tarde o para una cena, el Vogue es desde hace años el local predilecto de un público movido por la moda y las tendencias. El ambiente es elegante y clásico a la vez. La revista Vogue pone no sólo su nombre sino además una gran selección de fotografías de moda que allí se exponen.

Galereya

Studio 69

2004
Petrovka Street 27
Tverskoe

www.novikovgroup.ru

This restaurant owes its popularity to various exhibitions of high-gloss photography and modern art. Its ambience is modern and exquisite with dark wood, light columns, private areas with sofas, and a remarkable bar. For the summertime, there's a sheltered patio in the quiet courtyard.

Wechselnde Ausstellungen mit Hochglanzfotografie und moderner Kunst sind ein Grund für die Beliebtheit dieses Restaurants. Das Ambiente ist modern und edel mit dunklem Holz, Lichtsäulen, Rückzugsbereichen mit Sofas und einer in Szene gesetzten Bar. Im Sommer gibt es eine geschützte Veranda im ruhigen Innenhof.

Ce restaurant jouit d'une grande popularité grâce aux expositions de photographies sur papier glacé et d'art moderne qui y sont régulièrement organisées. L'atmosphère est moderne et raffinée, avec du bois sombre, des colonnes de lumière, des espaces en retrait avec des canapés et un bar élégamment mis en scène. En été, il y a une véranda couverte dans une tranquille cour intérieure.

Si el restaurante es uno de los predilectos se debe en parte a las exposiciones de fotografías con brillo y arte moderno. El ambiente es moderno y elegante y está vestido de maderas oscuras, columnas luminosas, espacios de recogimiento con sofás y un bar haciendo de centro. En verano se puede disfrutar de la terraza protegida en el tranquilo patio interior.

Shatush

Konstantin Chernyavsky

2004
Gogolevsky Boulevard 17
Khamovniki

www.shatush.ru

This establishment owes its success to its discretion. A shroud of darkness protects the patrons from curious glances. Its few glass surfaces are intense tones of blue; bright leather seats are combined with dark wood. Serving as both a bar and a club, this Chinese restaurant is an attraction for night revelers.

Die Diskretion des Ortes ist sein Erfolg. Einhüllende Dunkelheit schützt den Gast vor neugierigen Blicken. Die wenigen Glasflächen sind in intensivsten Blautönen gehalten, helle Ledersitze werden mit dunklem Holz kombiniert. Das chinesische Restaurant ist als Bar und Club gleichzeitig Anziehungspunkt für Nachtschwärmer.

La discrétion du lieu en fait son succès. Une obscurité enveloppante protège l'hôte des regards indiscrets. Les rares surfaces de verre sont teintées d'un bleu intense, le cuir clair des sièges est associé à du bois sombre. Le restaurant chinois, qui est à la fois bar et club, est un pôle d'attraction pour les noctambules.

El éxito del lugar es la discreción. La oscuridad envuelve a los clientes protegiéndoles de las miradas curiosas. Las interminables superficies de vidrio se han mantenido en tonos azul intenso, y los asientos de piel se combinan con la madera oscura. El restaurante chino se transforma en centro de atención como bar y club para los amantes de la noche.

Vanil

Yury Andreev

2001
Ostozhenka Street 1
Khamovniki

www.eatout.ru
www.novikovgroup.ru

The entry area is dominated by an oversized semicircle serving as both reception and bar. The ornamental graphics on the glass surfaces—just one of many details in the Vanil—and bright, crème-colored accents give the place an exclusive character.

Der Eingangsbereich wird von einem überdimensionalen Halbrund dominiert, das gleichzeitig Rezeption und Bar ist. Die ornamentale Graphik auf den Glasflächen, nur eines von vielen Details im Vanil, gibt ihm zusammen mit hellen, cremefarbenen Möbeln und Vorhängen seinen exklusiven Charakter.

L'entrée est occupée par un demi-cercle surdimensionné qui fait fonction à la fois de réception et de bar. Le graphique ornemental sur les surfaces vitrées – un détail parmi d'autres au Vanil – lui confère, en combinaison avec des meubles et rideaux clairs, couleur crème, son caractère exclusif.

El espacio de la entrada está dominado por un semicírculo supradimensional, que hace las funciones de recepción y bar al mismo tiempo. Las gráficas ornamentales sobre las superficies de vidrio, uno de los muchos detalles de Vanil, transmiten un carácter exclusivo que se ve acentuado además por muebles y cortinajes de tonos crema.

Arkhitektor

Albina Nazimova

2003
Malaya Nikitskaya Street 20
Presnenskoe

Jazz concerts and cabarets take place on the small stage of the Arkhitektor. Oversized lampshades, pictures, and a fireplace made of natural stone dominate the central area. Its clientele includes architects and artists, giving the place a pleasantly "democratic" atmosphere.

Jazzkonzerte und Chansons werden auf der kleinen Bühne des Arkhitektor geboten. Überdimensionale Lampenschirme, Gemälde und der Natursteinkamin prägen den zentralen Raum. Zum Publikum gehören Architekten und Künstlervolk, dabei herrscht eine angenehm „demokratische" Stimmung.

Sur la petite scène de l'Arkhitektor ont lieu des concerts de jazz et des soirées chansons. D'immenses abat-jour, des tableaux et une cheminée en pierre naturelle marquent l'espace central. Le public est composé d'une tribu d'artistes et d'architectes, parmi lesquels règne une ambiance agréablement « démocratique ».

Su pequeño escenario deleita con conciertos de Jazz y Chansons. La sala central está dominada por las enormes pantallas de lámparas, cuadros y una chimenea de piedra. Entre su público se encuentran arquitectos y personajes del mundo artístico, que se envuelven del ambiente "democrático".

Pavillion

Brano Shouz

2005
Bol. Patriarshy Lane 7
Presnenskoe

www.restoran-oblomov.ru

Room-high arc-shaped windows offer a view of the Patriarch Pond, where the pavilion of the restaurant is located. A gallery surrounds the main hall, where photos of androgynous models and stars decorate the walls. It's definitely the place to see and be seen.

Raumhohe Bogenfenster geben den Blick auf den Patriarch-Teich frei, an dem der Pavillon des Restaurants steht. Der Hauptsaal wird von einer Galerie umrahmt. Fotografien androgyner Models und Stars zieren die Wände. Hier will man sehen und gesehen werden.

Les grandes fenêtres en arcade ouvrent la vue sur l'étang du Patriarche au bord duquel se trouve le pavillon du restaurant. La salle à manger principale est entourée d'une galerie. Des photographies de mannequins androgynes et de stars décorent les murs. Ici, il faut voir et être vu.

Las ventanas de arcada de suelo a techo lanzan la vista al estanque del Patriarca, en el que está ubicado el pabellón del restaurante. El salón principal está rodeado por una galería. Las paredes están decoradas con fotografías de estrellas y modelos andróginos. Aquí se desea ver y ser visto.

Villa

Yury Andreev

2004
Myasnitskaya Street 48
Meshchanskoe

www.villa.su

Its perfect 1920s art deco style gives this restaurant an exquisite and genuine character. The finest mosaics, mostly in gold, have been incorporated in the fireplace, the ceiling, and the staircase. Heavy red curtains separate the private rooms on the upper floor.

Ganz im Art déco-Stil der 20er Jahre gibt sich das Restaurant edel und gediegen. Feinste Mosaike, hauptsächlich in Gold gehalten, sind an Kamin, Decke und dem Treppenaufgang verarbeitet. Schwere rote Vorhänge trennen im oberen Stock die einzelnen Separees.

Le restaurant a opté pour une solide élégance, tout à fait dans le style Art Déco des années 20. De fines mosaïques, pour la plupart dorées, ornent la cheminée, le plafond et la montée de l'escalier. À l'étage supérieur, de lourds rideaux rouges séparent les box individuels.

El elegante y refinado restaurante ha optado por el Art Decó de los años 20. La chimenea, el techo y la subida a la escalera están revestidos de los más finos mosaicos, la mayoría en oro. En la planta superior pesadas cortinas rojas separan los reservados.

City Space Bar & Lounge

BBG-BBGM

2005
Kosmodamianskaya Embankment 52
Bldg. 6, 34th Floor
Paveletskaya

www.moscow.swissotel.com

High above the city on the 34th floor of the Swissôtel Krasnye Holmy, one can get a view of this city of millions. The 360-degree view is amazing. A DJ provides a relaxed atmosphere, although it's apt to turn into a bustling party as night approaches.

Hoch über der Stadt im 34. Stock des Swissôtel Krasnye Holmy blickt man vom Süden Moskaus auf die Millionenmetropole. Die 360°-Aussicht lädt zum Verweilen und Staunen ein. Ein DJ sorgt für entspannte Atmosphäre, zu späterer Stunde steigert sich die Stimmung gern zu einer ausgelassenen Party.

Dominant la ville au 34ème étage du Swissôtel Krasnye Holmy, du sud de Moscou, le client contemple cette grande métropole. La vue panoramique sur 360° invite à la détente et à l'émerveillement. Grâce au disk jockey, l'atmosphère est décontractée mais plus tard dans la soirée, l'ambiance de la fête devient plus turbulente.

Por encima de la ciudad, en el piso 34 del Swissôtel Krasnye Holmy se divisa desde el sur la metrópoli rusa. Las vistas de 360° invitan a dejarse asombrar y pasar el tiempo. El DJ se encarga de ofrecer un ambiente distendido, si bien, a medida que avanza la noche, la atmósfera adquiere un aire relajado de fiesta.

Suzy Wong

Evgeny Mitta, Giya Abramishvili

2005
Timura Frunze Street 11/34
Khamovniki

www.suzywongbar.ru

Mighty armchairs made of dark leather, fine materials, and floral ornaments invite customers to sit back and unwind. The brick walls of the tube-like room are lime-washed in simple white. Pop art pictures on the walls form a contrast to the antique-looking Asian cabinets and knick-knacks.

Mächtige Sessel aus dunklem Leder, edle Stoffe und florale Muster laden zum Fallenlassen ein. Die Ziegelwände des schlauchartigen Raumes sind simpel weiß getüncht. Hier hängen Pop Art-Bilder, die im Kontrast zu den alt anmutenden, asiatischen Kommoden und Accessoires stehen.

De larges fauteuils de cuir sombre, de riches étoffes et des motifs floraux sont parfaits pour se laisser aller. Les murs de brique de la salle, toute en longueur, sont simplement badigeonnés de blanc. Ici, des affiches pop art sont suspendues, contrastant avec les commodes et accessoires asiatiques à l'aspect antique.

Imponente sillones de piel oscura, telas nobles y motivos florales que invitan a dejarse llevar. Las paredes de ladrillo de la estancia en forma de túnel están pintadas de un simple blanco. En ellas cuelgan cuadros del Pop Art, creando un contraste con las cómodas y accesorios asiáticos de estilo antiguo.

Dental Clinic TBI
Healthcare Center

M. Khazanov Studio, S. Ploughnik, I.Topcheeva, A. Nagavitsyn, M. Khasanov
N. Kancheli, N. Grinberg (SE)

2000
Ostozhenka Street 6
Ostozhenka

www.tbistomatology.ru

The architecture of the clinic is just as clear, professional, and technological as modern dental practices with twinkling glass areas and lots of metal details. Nevertheless, the facility appears accommodating and friendly, blending into the historic architecture of the quarter.

Die Architektur der Klinik ist genauso klar, sachlich und technologisch wie moderne Zahnarztpraxen – mit glitzernden Glasflächen und vielen Metalldetails. Und dennoch sieht das Haus menschlich und freundlich aus und fügt sich organisch in die historische Bebauung des Viertels ein.

L'architecture de cette clinique est aussi claire, réaliste et technologique que les cabinets dentaires modernes – avec des surfaces de verre luisantes et de nombreux éléments en métal. La maison a cependant une apparence « humaine » et agréable et s'intègre de façon organique à la culture historique du quartier.

La arquitectura de la clínica es exactamente igual de clara, neutral y tecnológica que las modernas consultas de dentista. Superficies resplandecientes de vidrio y todo tipo de detalles en metal. Y aún así, el lugar transmite un ambiente humano y agradable y se integra perfectamente en las construcciones históricas del barrio.

142

Lokomotiv Stadium

Mosprojekt 4/Studio 6, A. Bokov, D. Bush, S. Chuklov, I. Babak
M. Libshin, P. Eremeev, A. Buzmakov (SE)

2002
Bol. Cherkizovskaya Street 125 a
North-East District

www.lokomotiv.ru
www.mniip.ru
www.bokov.info

Not only does this stadium meet international standards with maximum convenience for spectators and athletes, but it also has a bold steel-and-glass roof construction mounted to two outside pillars with wire cable. This assemblage makes the facility recognizable from afar.

Das Stadion entspricht nicht nur den internationalen Standards mit höchstem Komfort für Zuschauer und Spieler, sondern hat eine gewagte Stahlglas-Dachkonstruktion, die mit Drahtseilen an zwei Außenträgern befestigt ist. Dadurch bekommt das Gebäude sein von weitem erkennbares Erscheinungsbild.

Le stade ne correspond pas seulement aux standards internationaux en matière de confort pour les spectateurs et les joueurs, il présente également une toiture de verre et d'acier très hardie, fixée par des câbles d'acier à deux pylônes extérieurs. Ceci confère à cette construction une silhouette que l'on reconnaît de loin.

Además de corresponder a los estándares internacionales de confort para espectadores y jugadores, el estadio cuenta con una atrevida cubierta de vidrio y acero fijada con cables metálicos a dos pilones exteriores. Con ello el edificio adquiere una figura reconocible a los lejos.

Aquapark

Sergej Kiselev
V. Travush, I. Schvartsman (SE)

2002
Golubinskaya Street
Jasenevo

www.sk-p.ru

This complex with indoor pool, recreational pool, bowling, fitness center, and a number of cafés is located right where the city meets the countryside. Its flat, step-like shapes and shell-shaped aluminum roof allow it to blend organically into the landscape.

Der Komplex mit Schwimmhalle, Erholungsbad, Bowling, Fitnesszentrum und mehreren Cafés befindet sich an der Grenze zwischen Stadt und Land. Dank seiner flachen, stufenartigen Formen und des muschelartigen Aluminiumdaches fügt er sich organisch in die Landschaft ein.

Ce complexe comprenant une piscine, des bains de relaxation, un bowling, un centre de culturisme et plusieurs cafés, se situe à la frontière entre la ville et la campagne. Grâce à ses formes plates et étagées et à son toit en aluminium en forme de coquillage, il se fond organiquement dans le paysage.

En la frontera entre el campo y la ciudad está ubicado este complejo que cuenta con piscina cubierta, baños de relajación, bolera, gimnasio y diversas cafeterías. Sus formas planas y escalonadas y el techo de aluminio en forma de concha permiten que el lugar se funda armoniosamente en el entorno.

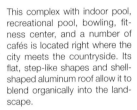

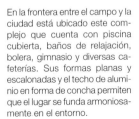

Ice Palace

Mosprojekt 4/Studio 6, A. Bokov, D. Bush, V. Valujskiy
M. Kelman, P. Eremeev, B. Travush (SE)

2003
Krylatskaya Street 16
Krylatskoe

www.ice-palace.ru
www.mniip.ru
www.bokov.info

This facility owes its striking silhouette—not unlike that of a shellfish—to its suspended roof construction. The enormous roof covers functionally divided ice slabs measuring three acres that enable 300 athletes to train simultaneously.

Der hängenden Dachkonstruktion verdankt die Sportstätte ihre markante, einem Schalentier ähnliche Silhouette. Unter dem riesigen Dach befinden sich funktional strukturierte Eisflächen von 12.000 m², die das gleichzeitige Training von bis zu 300 Sportlern ermöglichen.

Ce complexe sportif doit sa silhouette prononcée, ressemblant à un crustacé, à sa toiture suspendue. Sous cette immense toiture se trouvent des patinoires à la structure fonctionnelle sur une surface de 12.000 m², qui permettent à presque 300 sportifs de s'entraîner simultanément.

La estructura del techo colgante otorga al centro deportivo una silueta característica, semejante a un molusco. Bajo el enorme techo están ubicados los 12.000 m² de pistas de hielo, concebidas de forma funcional que ofrecen la posibilidad de entrenar a 300 deportistas a la vez.

Tennis Center Olympic Star

A. Asadov, A. Larin, A. Rozhdestwenskij, A. A. Asadov, Y. Mironova
A. Nebytov, A. Natarov, E. Kosygin, G. Marova (SE)

2002
Rublevskoe Chausse 10
Kuntsevo

www.olympicstar.ru
www.asadov.ru

The tennis center is embedded in the topography: An indoor swimming pool, fitness center, and sports hall are nestled inside a hill and are accessible through the oval entry in its middle. Its walkable green roof has tennis courts and three glass skylights that allow daylight into the building.

Das Zentrum ist in die Topographie eingebettet: Schwimmbad, Fitnessclub und Sporthalle befinden sich in einem Hügel und sind durch den ovalen Eingang in seiner Mitte erreichbar. Auf dem begehbaren grünen Dach findet man die Tennisplätze, sowie drei Glashauben, die Tageslicht in das Gebäude lassen.

Le centre est enchâssé dans la topographie du lieu : piscine, club de fitness et gymnase se trouvent sur une colline et sont accessibles par l'entrée ovale du milieu. Sur le toit végétalisé praticable, il y a les courts de tennis ainsi que trois lanterneaux qui laissent pénétrer la lumière dans le bâtiment.

El centro se ha fundido en la topografía del lugar. La piscina, gimnasio y pabellón de deportes están integrados en una colina y a ellos se accede a través de una entrada oval. Sobre el techo transitable se encuentran las pistas de tenis y tres cubiertas de vidrio que proporcionan luz diurna al edificio.

to shop . mall
retail
showrooms

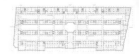

GUM Renovation

Mosprojekt 2, P. Andreev, S. Pavlov
V. Parnes (SE)

2002
Krasnaya Place 3
Red Square

www.gum.ru

Following its careful renovation, one of the oldest and prettiest shopping passages of Moscow now has a new level underneath its glass roof. This former administrative level used to be inaccessible to the public; today, light new bridges link the galleries with boutiques and cafés.

Mit der sorgfältigen Renovierung bekam eine der ältesten und schönsten Moskauer Einkaufspassagen eine neue Ebene unter dem gläsernen Dach. Früher war diese Verwaltungsebene für das Publikum unzugänglich. Heute verbinden leichte neue Brücken die Galerien mit Boutiquen und Cafés.

Lors d'une rénovation soignée, l'une des plus anciennes et des plus belles galeries marchandes de Moscou s'est vu adjoindre un nouvel étage sous la verrière du toit. Auparavant, cet étage réservé à l'administration était fermé au public. Désormais, de nouveaux ponts très légers relient les galeries avec des boutiques et des cafés.

Gracias a la cuidada renovación, una de las galerías más antiguas y hermosas de Moscú bajo techo acristalado ha alcanzado una nueva dimensión. En el pasado, esta superficie de oficinas de la administración no estaba abierta al público. Hoy las pequeñas pasarelas vinculan las galerías con boutiques y cafeterías.

Christian Louboutin Boutique

Lab for Virtual Architecture, A. Karpova, D. Kulish (Interior Design)

2003
Petrovka Street 5
Center

www.christianlouboutin.fr
www.labva.ru

Extravagant, provocative, and sophisticated, yet a bit nostalgic and symbolic at the same time—just like the shoes by the famous Parisian shoe designer themselves—effectively describe his Moscow boutique. It comes, of course, with a red carpet for those famous red soles.

Extravagant und provokativ, modern, aber gleichzeitig ein bisschen nostalgisch und symbolträchtig – so wie die Schuhe des berühmten Pariser Schuhdesigner selbst – ist seine Moskauer Boutique. Selbstverständlich mit einem rotem Teppich für die berühmten roten Sohlen.

Extravagant et provocateur, moderne mais aussi avec un brin de nostalgie et beaucoup de symboles – à l'instar de ses chaussures – c'est ainsi que se présente le magasin moscovite du célèbre créateur parisien de chaussures. Avec, bien entendu, un tapis rouge pour les fameuses semelles rouges.

Extravagante, provocativo, moderno pero un tanto nostálgico y a la vez cargado de simbolismo. Al igual que los zapatos del prestigioso diseñador de calzado parisino, así es su boutique de Moscú. Y naturalmente con una alfombra roja para las famosas suelas rojas.

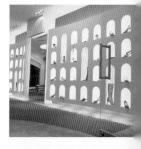

Novinsky Passage

Architecture Bureau A-B, A. Savin, M. Labazov, A. Tscheltsov

2003
Novinsky Boulevard 31
Center

www.novinsky.ru

The shopping mall is located on the first three floors of a large office building and contrasts with the monumental architecture of the latter. It is a place where light, air, and transparency prevail. Each entry area has its own color and the lighting behind the glass walls makes for a cool, club-like atmosphere.

Das Einkaufszentrum befindet sich in den ersten drei Etagen eines großen Bürohauses und steht im Kontrast zu dessen monumentaler Architektur. Hier herrschen Licht, Luft und Transparenz. Jeder Eingangsbereich hat seine eigene Farbe und die Beleuchtung hinter den gläsernen Wänden schafft eine coole Club-Atmosphäre.

Ce centre commercial occupe les trois premiers étages d'un grand immeuble de bureaux, en contraste absolu avec son architecture monumentale. Ici règnent la lumière, l'air et la transparence. Chaque zone d'entrée a sa propre couleur et l'éclairage derrière des cloisons vitrées crée une atmosphère de club très cool.

El centro comercial está ubicado en las tres primeras plantas del gran edificio de oficinas y se muestra en contraste con su monumental arquitectura. Aquí dominan la luz, el aire y la transparencia. Cada una de las entradas tiene su propio color y la iluminación tras las paredes acristaladas emana un fresco ambiente de club.

Arsenal

ABD Architects Ltd., B. Levjant, N. Sidorova, D. Lorentz

1997
Presnenskiy Val 36
Presnya

www.abdcom.ru

This store makes one forget how dangerous its displayed merchandise is. The exquisite glow of its granite surfaces, effectively highlighted behind the glass display cases, makes the knives, rifles, and guns look like simple museum exhibits. The only thing missing is the "Please do not touch" sign.

In diesem Laden vergisst man, wie gefährlich die ausgestellten Waren sind. Im edlen Glanz der Granitflächen, effektvoll beleuchtet hinter den Glasvitrinen, sehen die Messer, Gewehre und Pistolen wie reine Museumsexponate aus. Es fehlen bloß die Tafeln „Bitte nicht berühren!".

Dans ce magasin, on oublie combien les articles exposés sont dangereux. Dans l'éclat distingué du granit, sous un éclairage théâtral derrière des vitrines de verre, les couteaux, fusils et pistolets ressemblent à d'authentiques pièces de musée. Il ne manque plus que les écriteaux « Prière de ne pas toucher ».

En este comercio se tiende a olvidar lo peligrosos que son los artículos expuestos. En la elegante brillantez de las superficies de granito y con una iluminación cargada de efecto detrás de las vitrinas, se presentan cuchillos y armas como si de objetos de museo se tratase. Ya casi sólo faltan los carteles de "por favor no tocar".

Design Center ARTPLAY

S. Desyatov

2004
Timura Frunze Street 11/34
Khamovniki

www.artplay.ru

Constructed in 1875 and named in the honor of Rosa Luxemburg after the revolution, the "Red Rosa" textile factory has been renovated and converted into a design center. On an area of 2.5 acres, one can find numerous architectural offices, design boutiques, showrooms, and art exhibitions.

Die nach der Revolution zu Ehren von Rosa Luxemburg benannte, 1875 erbaute Textilfabrik „Rote Rosa" wurde restauriert und zu einem Design-Zentrum umgewandelt. Auf einer Fläche von 10.000 m² findet man zahlreiche Architektenbüros, Design-Boutiquen, Showrooms und Kunstausstellungen.

La fabrique de textile « Rosa rouge », construite en 1875 et appelée ainsi après la Révolution en l'honneur de Rosa Luxemburg, a été restaurée et transformée en centre de création. Sur une surface de 10.000 m² se trouvent de nombreux bureaux d'architectes, des boutiques design, des salles de présentation et des expositions d'art.

La fábrica de textiles fundada en 1875 obtuvo el nombre de "Rosa roja" tras las revolución en honor a Rosa Luxemburgo y posteriormente fue restaurada y convertida en un centro de diseño. En una superficie de 10.000 m² se concentran numerosas oficinas de arquitectos, boutiques de diseño, salas expositoras y exposiciones de arte.

Cappellini

Atrium, A. Nadtochy, V. Butko, O.Sokolova

2001
Leningradsky Prospect 52
North-West District

www.cappellini.it
www.atrium.ru

In an L-shaped room of this furniture boutique, a spatial composition has been created of four plateaus that flow into each other. Each plateau has its own color solution. Three stairs made of different materials—geometrical sculptures unto themselves—add a dynamic touch.

In einem L-förmigen Raum der Möbelboutique wurde eine räumliche Komposition aus vier ineinander fließenden Ebenen geschaffen. Jedes Plateau bekommt seine eigene farbliche Lösung. Drei Treppen aus verschiedenen Materialien bringen Dynamik ins Spiel und wirken wie geometrische Skulpturen.

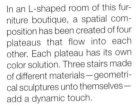

Dans une pièce en L de ce magasin de meubles, l'espace a été agencé en une succession fluide de quatre niveaux. Chaque plateforme bénéficie de sa propre couleur. Trois escaliers dans des matériaux différents dynamisent l'ensemble et font figure de sculptures géométriques.

En una sala en forma de L de esta boutique de mobiliario se ha creado una composición de cuatro niveles fundidos entre sí. Cada plataforma tiene su propio tono. Tres escaleras de diversos materiales levantadas como esculturas geométricas se encargan de dar dinamismo al lugar.

Trade Center Semenovskiy

Lyzlov Architectural Studio, N. Lyzlov, S. Kaverina, A. Krasnov
G. Kalchuk (SE)

2001
Boljshaja Semenovskaya Street 28
Izmailovo

www.lyzlov.ru

This modern structure of glass, metal, and brick presents a revival of the tradition of the urban department store in the style of the 1920s while maintaining the scale and structural quality of turn-of-the-century architecture. Light effects highlight its expressive formal composition.

Das moderne Gebäude aus Glas, Metall und Backstein ist eine Wiederbelebung der Tradition der großstädtischen Kaufhausarchitektur in der Formensprache der 20er Jahre und im Maßstab und in der baulichen Qualität der Jahrhundertwende. Die expressive formale Komposition wurde mit Lichteffekten akzentuiert.

Ce bâtiment moderne de verre, de métal et de briques fait revivre l'architecture traditionnelle des grands magasins des villes dans le langage des formes des années 20, aux dimensions et dans la qualité de construction du tournant du siècle. Cette composition formelle très expressive est accentuée par des effets de lumière.

El moderno edificio de vidrio, metal y ladrillo revive formalmente la tradición de la arquitectura de los grandes almacenes de los años 20, y sigue fiel a la calidad constructiva del cambio de siglo. La expresiva composición ha sido acentuada con efectos de luz.

Mercedes Benz Center Avilon

A. Asadov, A. A. Asadov
A. Nebytov, N. Kancheli, E. Vladimirov (SE)

2002
Volgogradsky Prospect 43 a
South-East District

www.avilon.ru
www.asadov.ru

Despite the carmaker's strict policies for all its facilities, this Moscow subsidiary has been given its own very individual appearance; in Russia, Mercedes is not just regarded as a car brand, but as the symbol of a dream. This symbolic meaning is exhibited by architecture, light and color.

Trotz der strengen Vorschriften des Konzerns für alle seine Einrichtungen bekam diese Moskauer Niederlassung ihre ganz individuelle Erscheinung, weil Mercedes in Russland nicht nur eine Automarke, sondern Symbol eines Traums ist. Und dies wurde durch Architektur, Licht und Farbe ausgedrückt.

Malgré les instructions très strictes de l'entreprise quant à l'aménagement de ses succursales, celle de Moscou bénéficie d'une image très individuelle car Mercedes en Russie n'est pas seulement une marque automobile, mais aussi le symbole d'un rêve. C'est ce qu'expriment ici l'architecture, la lumière et la couleur.

A pesar de las estrictas normas que marca la multinacional para todas sus representaciones, la filial de Moscú ha adoptado un aspecto especialmente individual, ya que Mercedes en Rusia no sólo es una marca de coches sino el símbolo de un sueño, que se expresa a través de la arquitectura, la luz y los colores.

Trade & Entertaining Center Varshavskiy

A. A. Chernikhov' Design and Architecture Studio, A. A. Chernikhov,
M. Ruben, N. Zhorova
I. Kanikaev (SE)

2003
Varshavskoe Chausse 78 b
Chertanovo

The center adds a striking accent to Moscow's longest and architecturally most inconspicuous freeway. Its façades are made up of shifted, wavy, twisted and multi-colored surfaces—like something out of a children's game. This game continues on into the inside the building even though the overall structure remains clear and functional.

Das Zentrum setzt einen markanten Akzent an der längsten und architektonisch gesichtslosesten Schnellstraße Moskaus. Seine Fassaden bestehen aus versetzten, gewellten und gedrehten bunten Flächen – wie aus einem Kinderspiel. Dieses Spiel setzt sich fort im Inneren des Gebäudes, und doch bleibt die gesamte Struktur klar und funktional.

Ce centre est un élément particulièrement frappant sur la voie express la plus longue et la plus anonyme, au plan architectural, de Moscou. Ses façades sont constituées de surfaces de couleur décalées, ondulées et tournées – comme dans un jeu d'enfant. Ce jeu se poursuit à l'intérieur du bâtiment où la structure générale reste pourtant nette et fonctionnelle.

El centro marca un llamativo acento en la autovía más larga y arquitectónicamente más inexpresiva de Moscú. Sus fachadas se componen de multicolores superficies superpuestas, retorcidas y onduladas que parecen un juego infantil. El juego se amplía a los interiores del edificio, manteniendo una entera estructura clara y funcional.

Quadro

Reserve, Vladimir Plotkin, Irina Deeva, Yu. Kuzin

2003
Kutuzovsky Prospect 88
Fili

www.reserve.ru

This glass structure has the effect of a gigantic display window, showing the inside goings-on of the building while at the same time reflecting the outside world. Light, metal, and glass interact with dexterity in the atrium; the buoyant spiral staircase adds a unique accent.

Der gläserne Körper wirkt wie ein riesiges Schaufenster, das das Innenleben des Gebäudes zeigt und gleichzeitig die Außenwelt spiegelt. Licht, Metall und Glas spielen auch im Atrium gemeinsam eine virtuose Partie. Und die schwungvolle Wendeltreppe setzt einen effektvollen Akzent.

Le corps de bâtiment en verre ressemble à une immense vitrine montrant la vie intérieure du bâtiment et reflétant simultanément le monde extérieur. Lumière, métal et verre se donnent magistralement la réplique dans l'atrium. L'escalier en colimaçon élancé accentue l'effet général.

Los cuerpos acristalados crean el efecto de un enorme escaparate que muestra la vida interior del edificio reflejando a la vez el mundo exterior. La luz, el metal y el vidrio tienen también un papel virtuoso en el atrio. Mientras, la dinámica escalera de caracol crea un acento cargado de efecto.

Europark

ABD Architects Ltd., B. Levjant, B. Stuchebrjukov, S. Djabrailov, E. Gavrilova

2005
Rublevskoe Chausse 62
Kuntsevo

www.abdcom.ru

This multi-colored, 1,150-foot-long iron snake wending along the highway only appears unapproachable and warehouse-like from the outside. On the inside, it appears as a clearly structured arcade—with lots of daylight generously flowing in from its slanted roof windows.

Die 350 m lange, bunte eiserne Schlange entlang der Autobahn wirkt nur von außen so verschlossen und lagerartig. Im Inneren sieht sie wie eine klar strukturierte Passage aus – mit viel Tageslicht, das großzügig von den querliegenden Dachfenstern fließt.

Vu de l'extérieur, le serpent d'acier multicolore qui s'étire sur 350 m le long de l'autoroute ressemble à un entrepôt fermé. De l'intérieur, il se révèle être un passage clairement structuré – recevant beaucoup de lumière du jour qui pénètre généreusement par les lucarnes transversales.

La multicolor serpiente de acero de 350 m a lo largo de la autopista parece cerrada y en forma de almacén sólo desde el exterior. Por dentro se presenta como un pasaje estructurado con abundante luz diurna que resbala ostentosa por las ventanas transversales.

5th Avenue

ABD Architects Ltd., B. Levyant, B. Stuchebrjukov, A. Barkalov

2004
Marshalla Biryuzova Street 32
Krylatskoe

www.abdcom.ru

A reduction in forms and colors turns this shopping mall into a great aesthetic experience. The black crosses of the escalators add expressive accents to the brightly-lit area of the atrium; the white galleries and the red supports are interwoven into geometric ornaments.

Reduktion der Formen und Farben machen dieses Einkaufszentrum zum großen ästhetischen Erlebnis. Die schwarzen Kreuze der Rolltreppen setzen expressive Akzente im lichtdurchfluteten Raum des Atriums, wobei sich die weißen Galerien und die roten Stützen zu geometrischen Ornamenten verflechten.

Par la réduction des formes et des couleurs, ce centre commercial est une grande expérience esthétique. Le croisement noir des escaliers mécaniques est un élément expressif dans cet atrium inondé de lumière, tandis que les galeries blanches et les piliers rouges constituent des ornements géométriques entrelacés.

La reducción en las formas y los colores del centro comercial convierten al lugar en una verdadera experiencia estética. Los entrecruzados negros de las escaleras mecánicas marcan acentos expresivos en un atrio inundado de luz. Al espectáculo se unen galerías blancas y pilares rojos que entrelazan ornamentos geométricos.

Dream House

Murray O'Laoire Architects

2005
Rublevo-Uspenskoe Chausse 85/1
Barvicha Village

www.dreamhouse.ru
www.murrayolaoire.com

This complex—with furniture boutiques and stores selling everything necessary to make a dream home a reality—has truly earned its name. Two individual brick buildings are linked by a triangular glass roof in such a way that a spectacular atrium is created between them.

Der Komplex mit Möbel-Boutiquen und Läden mit allem, was man braucht, um sein Traumhaus zu verwirklichen, trägt seinen Namen vollkommen zu Recht. Zwei einzelne Backsteingebäude sind mit einem dreieckigen Glasdach so verbunden, dass zwischen ihnen ein spektakuläres Atrium entsteht.

Ce complexe abritant des boutiques de meubles et des magasins vendant tout ce qu'il faut pour réaliser son rêve de maison individuelle, porte son nom à merveille. Deux immeubles de brique séparés sont reliés par une toiture de verre triangulaire de façon à créer entre eux un spectaculaire atrium.

Con razón lleva su nombre este complejo de boutiques de mobiliario y comercios. Aquí se encuentra todo lo necesario para hacer realidad el sueño del propio hogar. Los dos edificios independientes de ladrillo están unidos por un techo de vidrio triangular que abarca un atrio espectacular.

Index Architects / Designers

Index Architects / Designers

Index Architects / Designers

Index Structural Engineers

Index Districts

Photo Credits

Imprint

Copyright © 2007 teNeues Verlag GmbH & Co. KG, Kempen

Published by teNeues Publishing Group

teNeues Verlag GmbH + Co. KG
Am Selder 37
47906 Kempen, Germany
Phone: 0049-2152-916-0
Fax: 0049-2152-916-111

teNeues Publishing Company
16 West 22nd Street
New York, N.Y. 10010, USA
Phone: 001-212-627-9090
Fax: 001-212-627-9511

teNeues
International Sales Division
Speditionstraße 17
40211 Düsseldorf, Germany
Phone: 0049-211-994597-0
Fax: 0049-211-994597-40
E-mail: books@teneues.de

teNeues France S.A.R.L.
4, rue de Valence
75005 Paris, France
Phone: 0033-1-55 76 62 05
Fax: 0033-1-55 76 64 19

teNeues Publishing UK Ltd.
P.O. Box 402
West Byfleet, KT14 7ZF, UK
Phone: 0044-1932-403 509
Fax: 0044-1932-403 514

teNeues Iberica S.L.
c/ Velázquez, 57 6.° izda.
28001 Madrid, Spain
Phone: 0034-657-132133

teNeues
Representative Office Italy
Via San Vittore 36/1
20123 Milan, Italy
Phone: 0039-347-7640551

Press department: arehn@teneues.de
Phone: 0049-(0)2152-916-202, www.teneues.com

ISBN–10: 3-8327-9156-6
ISBN–13: 978-3-8327-9156-8

Bibliographic information published by Die Deutsche Bibliothek
Die Deutsche Bibliothek lists this publication in the Deutsche Nationalbibliografie;
detailed bibliographic data is available in the Internet at http://dnb.ddb.de

Concept of and:guides by Martin Nicholas Kunz
Edited by Katharina Feuer
Texts written by Irina Chipova
Layout: Katharina Feuer
Imaging & Pre-press, map: Jan Hausberg

Translation:
Artes Translations, Dr. Suzanne Kirkbright
English: Conan Kirkpatrick
Copy-editing: Carissa Kowalski
French: Brigitte Villaumié
Spanish: Carmen de Miguel

fusion-publishing stuttgart . los angeles www.fusion-publishing.com

Printed in Italy

Legend

and : guide

Size: 12.5 x 12.5 cm / 5 x 5 in. (CD-sized format)
192 pp., Flexicover
c. 200 color photographs and plans
Text in English, German, French, Spanish

Other titles in the
same series:

Amsterdam
ISBN: 3-8238-4583-7

Barcelona
ISBN: 3-8238-4574-8

Berlin, 2nd edition
ISBN: 3-8327-9155-8

Chicago
ISBN: 3-8327-9025-X

Copenhagen
ISBN: 3-8327-9077-2

Hamburg
ISBN: 3-8327-9078-0

Hong Kong
ISBN: 3-8327-9125-6

London
ISBN: 3-8238-4572-1

Los Angeles
ISBN: 3-8238-4584-5

Mexico City
ISBN: 3-8327-9157-4

Munich
ISBN: 3-8327-9024-1

New York, 2nd edition
ISBN: 3-8327-9126-4

Paris
ISBN: 3-8238-4573-X

Prague
ISBN: 3-8327-9079-9

San Francisco
ISBN: 3-8327-9080-2

Shanghai
ISBN: 3-8327-9023-3

Tokyo
ISBN: 3-8238-4569-1

Vienna
ISBN: 3-8327-9026-8

teNeues